ALIEN
SPIRIT OF N

RONALD RAYNER

BLACKTHORN PUBLISHING

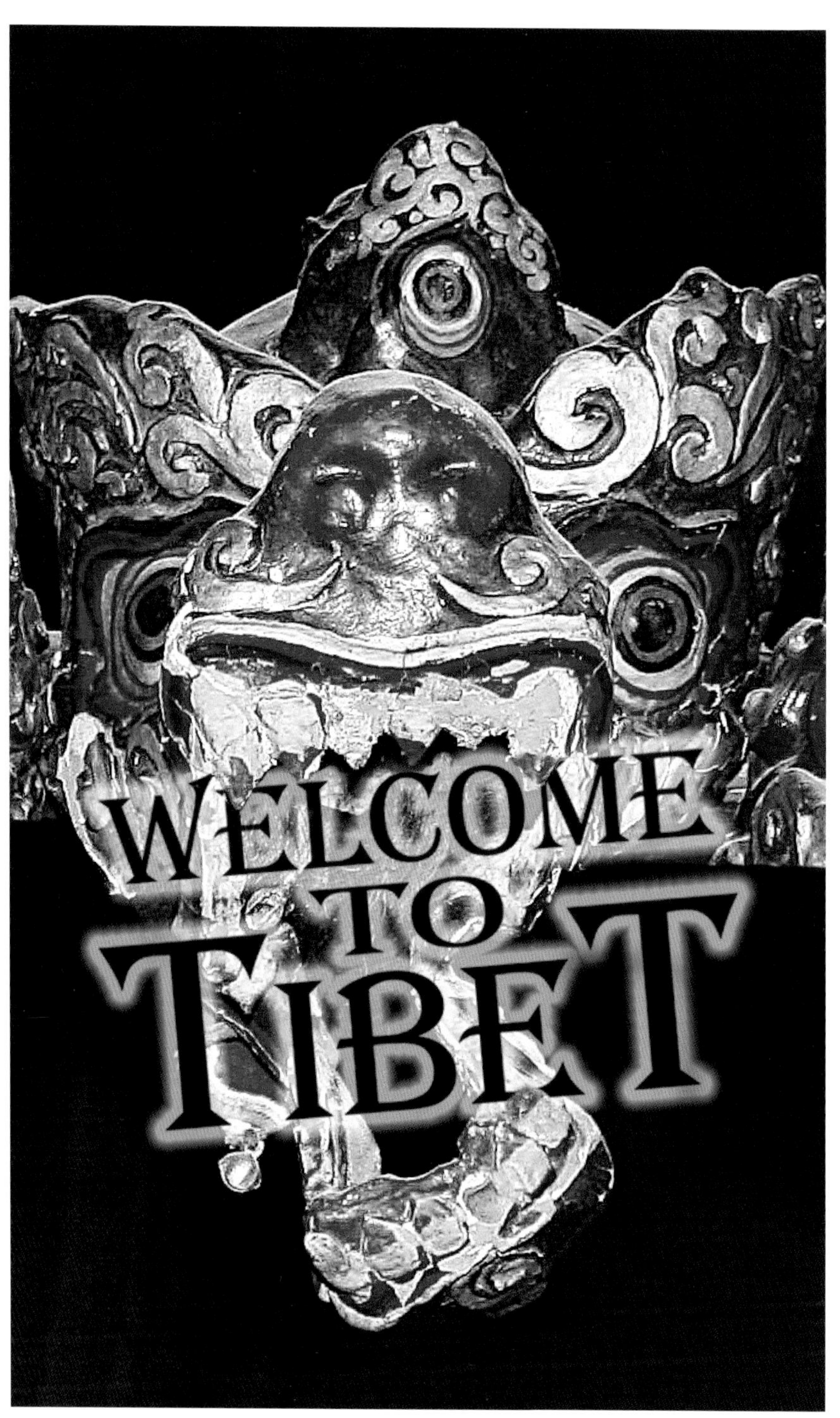

Uncovering the Secrets of Tibet

Aliens in Tibet

The photograph shows a figure of an Alien carved on a Yak jawbone, found by Craig Allen Rayner in a cave at a secret location in Tibet, whilst on his way to Everest. The same figure was painted on the cave wall. This figure supports a legend by Tibetan Monks, who carry out Sky Burials on remote mountain locations, reporting sightings of strange craft and robotic figures, apparently examining rock falls and completely ignoring the presence of any passing monk with a body strapped to his back.

UK DISTRIBUTOR
Add Design
Leiston Enterprise Centre
Eastlands Industrial Estate
Leiston, Suffolk IP16 4US
United Kingdom
Telephone: (UK) 0845-6436395
E-Mail: info@add-design.co.uk

ISBN 978-0-9557906-4-5

PUBLISHER
Blackthorn Publishing Ltd
Suite 404, Albany House
324-326, Regent Street,
London W1B 3HH
United Kingdom

Design, Creation and Photography
By
Craig Allen Rayner

Spiritual Poetry
By
Sylvia Rayner

Printers:
Colt Press Ltd, Unit 7C Perry Road, Witham Essex CM8 3UD UK

The colour photographs in this book by Craig Allen Rayner, together with his artistic design, influenced by his time with Tibetan Monks, work with the text to bring out the spirit in the information conveyed by the author, and add to the world wide appeal of this unique work.

SPIRITUAL POETRY KOAN

Spiritual Poetry awakens those who seek after the truth in the world to an awareness that gives shape to things previously unknown, and a seat above the reaping of the whirlwind.

INDEX OF POEMS.

The author and publisher wish to thank Craig Allen Rayner for the extensive use of his collection of ancient artifacts from Tibet.

INDEX

Survivalist and Geographical Photographer Craig Allen Rayner on his way to Everest

Prologue

When I am writing my books, I do so quite unconcerned about what others might feel about my writing. This is because I set out to think outside 'the box', most of the time. My aim is to go forward treading everywhere, and anywhere. This is my way, proven by achieving successful results breaking through the window into that which is outside our normal senses, to discover what is inside the space within the space. This is why I live to write, more than I write to live.

We, all of us, inherit the ability within ourselves to become aware of almost everything that is outside our normal everyday senses. It is necessary only to develop the will to capture, memorise, and draw those moments of real insight into ourselves in order to move forwards and look at life in a whole new way, where we will discover that everything really is connected to what we are and what we can see.

The starting point is to look beyond the normal ways of knowing, which is simply walking around and observing. What we must learn to do is to walk around the subject, absorb our self into that subject, until we achieve that moment of mystical insight that will tell us everything about the subject, which is the way mysteries are revealed.

This is the path along which we can transcend our normal nature, and where we can begin to see and understand 'meaningful coincidences in time', those secret connections that most people perceive as unrelated events; but to us, this is a window into future time. All this and much more you will find revealed in this book, 'Alien Monk. Spirit of Nostradamus'. Everything I have written, I believe to be true. Let those who have eyes to see, let them see!

With great pleasure,

Ronald Rayner.

London, 14th April, 2010.

Best Wishes from Craig Rayner.

CHAPTER 1

ALIEN MONK

In the beginning, the mind of early man was hard wired to the principle of wanting to know the future, whereas the thinking and reasoning capacity of modern man is confined mainly to the world of appearances only. The reason ancient man wanted to know or be able to calculate an outcome of an event before it occurred is because it was an important tool for survival. To this end man sought the ability to see into the future using, Shaman, Mystics, Witch Doctors, Astrology, Magic, Palmistry, Fortune Telling; the list is extensive.

I have spent a lifetime in the study of supposed methods or systems for foretelling the future, only to discover that ninety five percent of methods used by their practitioners are the fanciful imaginings of those who are deluding themselves or grasping at straws, rather than face up to the confining restrictions of truth.

The only glimmer of hope that shone through the darkness in my research was the accuracy of looking into the future using different methods of scrying. These are systems of divination used by different cultures two thousand years in the past. Revelations from my initial experiments proved accurate beyond my expectations; very promising indeed. I qualify my enthusiasm by explaining that I was looking at planet earth, plus areas on the planet, and in the cosmos, for disasters that might strike planet earth and have a dramatic influence on food production in the future, or on the very survival of mankind. I was not looking into the future for individuals. This is an area I have always avoided for fear of being labelled an 'airhead', and how that might damage my impeccable reputation for honesty and truth.

In my recent books in this series, I have recorded the results of my experiments in parapsychology using systems of scrying that have been well tried and tested over thousands of years by different cultures; practiced by their priestly class or mystics, in my usual factual unbiased manner. The sole purpose of the scrying ceremonies was to predict the future for weather events, or any catastrophe event such as volcanic activity, earthquakes, flooding, or any major catastrophe that might place their peoples in peril. Today, I am also looking for clues of possible intercontinental atomic warfare.

NOSTRADAMUS

In this book I propose to show how mysticism and science came together in equal importance for the development of mankind. I am also going to take a look into future time and space by scrying in the manner of Nostradamus. A Frenchman, and devout catholic. He is heralded as the most famous Seer of all time, who lived over four hundred years ago, and whose prophesies are mulled over and written about time and time again in the present day.

In my last book I successfully scried in the manner of the High Priests in the Temple of Solomon, using Wilson my skeleton dressed in a Urim and Thummin. This experiment followed on from my success in a previous scrying session in the manner of the early Druids, in which I used a Crystal Skull, Crystal Wand, and a Crystal Globe. These experiments enabled me to crack the code being used by Nostradamus when he was making his predictions.

I am going to demonstrate to readers how, by changing both their thinking and the way in which they look at everything around them, they can themselves become involved in future time, and make preparation for what lies ahead.

Meaningful Coincidences in Time

My starting point is to ask readers to begin noticing Meaningful Coincidences in Time. Synchronicity, for example, can be an instance of orderedness, a psychic event amalgamated to a physical event, joining together to become a meaningful coincidence in time, pertaining to an individual or individuals concerned. Unfortunately, these are not happenings that can become part of a scientific experiment because they cannot be measured or be shown to be part of certain regularity. We must ourselves be aware that when we reach out to connect with, and identify these events, we must not grab onto a skein of meaninglessness. It will be helpful if I give an actual example of such an event.

I was helping a young married man recover from a mental illness brought on by unexpectedly losing his job. When he was able to return to work, I went along with him to his local Job Centre to give support. On the way, we stopped to look in at the sale items in a local shop. When we arrived at the Job Centre there was a queue of people in front of us. While we were waiting, a lady appeared at a door near the counter, and came over to us. She asked my friend where he had bought the item in the box he was holding. After writing down the details, she asked my friend what his skills were. He told her he was a print finisher. The expression on her face changed to a big smile. I can help you she exclaimed, with joy. A job for a print finisher has just dropped onto my desk. He got the job. The parcel my friend was carrying attracted the Job Centre Manageress to him. The job for which he was qualified had just dropped onto her desk. This is a clear example of a meaningful coincidence in time that came to the rescue of a young family during a crisis in their lives.

Any event or phenomenon that is not explainable by known natural laws should be treated with caution. However, some such occurrences can be fairly and honestly described as paranormal, which is just another part of our far reaching mind. I would be the first person to advise anyone not to believe anything that cannot show clear repeatable scientific proof that it is real. However, as I have already explained, psychic experiences and mysticism are not repeatable in a laboratory. All I ask is that readers keep an open mind as we progress through this book.

On the surface, the events at the Job Centre appeared unrelated, however, what they were in reality, was a chain of events coming together in a person's favour. Happening for reasons that are difficult for people to either see or understand, but all part of a greater reality, and also serving as a good example of cause and effect coming together to the same end.

In modern times, experts from various fields of study are looking at the future, aided by unimaginably powerful computers. They study world economics; the availability of such essential commodities, as oil, food and water resources. Other experts strive to find out what is going on in rival foreign powers to ascertain whether their own government needs to change tack to remain in juxtaposition, or pull ahead of rival nations. With all this power at their disposal, governments are still unable to prevent world crisis; the world banking problem being a classic example. It is my own personal opinion, however, that mystics and seers like myself cannot be replaced by computers, which may come as a relief to some.

If you have ever thought about meaningful coincidences in time, it may be that such a coincidence that has drawn you to choose to read this book.

Mankinds Future Will Be Very Different from the Past

I am going to take you on an exciting journey in which you will read of prophesies laying out the troubled years that are ahead. Unique information and knowledge that may change both your conscious perspective, and understanding, in a way that will cause you to look at everything very differently in the future; insights that should enable you to prepare for what is coming. On the horizon lies a future that will be very different to that which people, in general, have experienced in the past. This is perhaps another reason why you have been drawn towards reading this book.

Everything in our Universe is Entangled in Time

It is likely that you will read about and understand events in a way that others find impossible to grasp. Many people will always remain blinded by the high walls surrounding their immovable comfort zone. This is why everything out there, in future time, will remain a mystery to the majority of people living in the world. This book will, however, reveal to you that there is much more in the world than most people are aware exists. As a result, ideas will come into your mind, images will form in your brain, working together to give you a glimpse of what is over the horizon. It will be helpful to now become alert to coincidences in time in your daily life, particularly everything that is positive and helpful to you, but it is imperative that you retain a positive attitude to everything in your daily life. This practice is all part of the processes of opening up one's mind.

Everything within our local universe, and galaxy, are entangled in time. From time past to present time, from present time to future time; reflecting back from future time to the present, in a process known as 'feedback'. Everything within the cosmos literally depending upon everything else around it. However, the latest discoveries by our scientist have revealed that stitched into the fabric of our universe is a tiny degree of uncertainty, an uncertainty that grows and grows. Nothing, therefore, is absolutely certain, and is the factor that fetches the unpredictability that is within the fabric of the universe, and enables evolution. Almost everything in our universe is cyclical, but scientists are only now uncovering the immense importance of the disasters caused by some of these cyclical events, calamities that can endanger life on the planet.

Cycles in the Universe Dictate the Future for Mankind on Planet Earth

Sixty five million year cycles, and multiples of sixty five million year cycles, have trigger mass extinction events. Multiples of five thousand years, to twenty and twenty five thousand years, reaching out to one hundred thousand year cycles, have triggered climate change. There have been twenty three cold periods in the past one hundred thousand years. All these events amounted to more than mere cold snaps. All developing very rapidly, and triggering changes in three dimensional space and time. Human destiny is very clearly mirrored in the stars. Weather events predicted from the results of my scrying experiments, are happening all across the globe.

Mystics, like myself, are few and rare, but we rctain the ability to see connections with eternal life. From time past to present time, and into future time. Events in future time are not entirely fixed, either for individuals or events on the planet. Individuals change futurc time for themselves by the manner in which they lead their lives. As for the planet, the cycle of movements are already determined and can be calculated years into the future, with the exception of the unexpected super nova or pole shift. A few of these cycles can be triggered by the way in which mankind uses or abuses the surface of the planet and its resources. Poison the seas and strip the land, and a global warming event will flip planet earth into an ice age that will wipe away most of human kind on the planet in as little as forty years. Calamities such as these are already on the horizon. The activities of man have now become part of global warming.

One of my studies in parapsychology, linked to my own favourite field of structuralism, explained as drawing out memories from time past into three dimensional space in present time, and vice versa, taught me the important roll the subconscious mind plays in every day life, and how it is possible to see into time past and the future, by expanding and developing personal thoughts. However, if we aim to achieve the step up to a much higher level of thinking, we must edit what we allow ourselves to see and hear because everything becomes imprinted and recorded in our memory banks, the filing system to which our brain constantly refers. Only then can our mind develop the capability required to join with all the fields permeating three dimensional space and time. We, all of us, possess the ability to connect with that which is delicate, subtle, and outside our normal senses; we just have to make the effort.

Alien face carved on rare Tibetan Red Garnet

Tibetan Protective Amulets

Hand carved Conch Shell of Tibetan Deity,
decorated with Silver and Turquoise

Ancient Prayer Wheel with Carved Prayer Stone

CHAPTER 2
SCRYING IN THE MANNER OF THE DRUID HIGH PRIESTS

In a previous book, 'The Voyages of Joseph of Avalon' [www.josephofavalon.com] I carried through the procedure of Scrying in the Manner used by the Druids in Britain two thousand years ago, a method of divination using a Crystal Skull, Crystal Wand, and Crystal Globe. I followed as closely as possible the methods used by the Druid High Priests at that time.

I placed a comfortable seat in the centre of a circle that no one should enter during the ceremony. I faced the chair towards the setting sun in the West. I took each of the objects I would be using to the edge of the circle and offered them in turn towards the North, the South, the East and the West. I then settled into my seat at the centre of the circle, said my prayer for protection whilst clasping my piece of the Rock of Calvary. My precious piece of Calvary presented to me by Sister Katerina, who tended the Altar of Crucifixion at the Holy Sepulchre in Jerusalem, when I was making my documentary 'Jerusalem'.

Sitting with the Crystal Skull in my lap, a pen and notebook at my side, I drifted into trance meditation to see the future for the Planet Earth.

Everything I saw was recorded in that Book, with the exception of the Banking Crisis. I saw the Banking Crisis trigger a fifty year cycle of economic decline for the whole of Europe and America, bringing with it civil unrest that parts of Europe and the USA have not witnessed since antiquity. Conversely, I saw that the Asian economies were into a fifty year cycle of economic uptrend, which will be brought to a stop by a calamitous earthquake under Tokyo, the Capital of Japan. The next halt come from a

Author, Ronald Rayner, scrying with one of the original of the seven crystal skulls in the manner of Druid High Priests.

war between China and its neighbours over water. I omitted the banking crisis from my book because I felt strongly that to draw attention to a banking crisis without positive proof would have been irresponsible, but nowhere near as irresponsible as the announcements on radio and television, that a major bank was running out of money, without first going to the British Prime Minister and Chancellor for advice on how to deal with such a serious matter, and the likely subsequent consequences that such an announcement on Radio and Television would have on the banking industries around the world, and the roll on effects to commerce and industry.

Scrying in the Manner of the High Priests at the Temple of Solomon

In the second book in the series, 'Joseph Escapes to Glastonbury' [www.josephescapes.com] I set out to scry in the manner of the High Priests in the ancient Temple of Solomon. This involved making a breast plate, as it was known, into which were inserted twelve precious and semi precious stones, as described in the Bible. However, since I am not a Jewish High Priest, and I did not want to offend the Jewish religion, I decided to remove myself one step from the proceedings by using Wilson, the family skeleton, who would be wearing a Urim and Thummin breastplate. We sat Wilson at the table to take an afternoon strawberry tea together with us to set the mood, before moving him onto his seat alongside mine in the garden facing the falling sun. Before proceeding I offered the Scull of Doom, the Armageddon Skull, and the Crystal Skull to the four corners of the earth, the North, the South, the East, and the West in turn. I then said my prayer for protection, while clasping my piece of Calvary, before entering trance meditation and proceeding to use each skull in turn in the scrying ceremony.

Everything I saw during that session was in vivid technicolour. I have recorded the results in my last book, 'Joseph Escapes to Glastonbury' [www.josephescapes.com] but it was not a pleasant experience, from the point where I saw the Skeleton of Doom striding the Earth and calling out to me. A feeling of being afraid came over me, and I felt anxious to come out of the trance, but no worse than many situations I had faced in the Army. However, I confronted my fear and kept going until the mirage evaporated. I endured a few unpleasant nights afterwards, before returning to my old optimistic self.

Author, Ronald Rayner, scrying in the manner of the High Priests in the Temple of Solomon, using Wilson the Skeleton wearing the Urim and Thummin.

SCRYING IN THE MANNER OF NOSTRADAMUS

For this book I decided to scry in the manner of the 'King of Scrying' Nostradamus, using the top of a human skull from a long dead Shaman. This I filled with water. I lit a candle and placed it in a position so that the flame of the candle reflected on to the water. Nostradamus would then enter into trance meditation, before recording everything he saw, as do I.

Wilson and I were seated in my garden in two comfortable chairs of the period of Nostradamus, facing the setting sun. In front of use was a small Singaporean wicker topped table, finished in real gold paint, with a circular plate glass top on which I set the shaman skull (from Craig Allen Rayner's collection) filled with spring water. Next to the top of the skull I set the face of the skull, and a gold wand to dip into the four quarters of the skull. I lit a candle beside the skull and placed it in position to reflect into the water. We were ready to proceed. I was set to peer through the curtain into the future for the planet in the manner of Nostradamus. I said my prayer for protection, and drifted into trance meditation clasping my piece of Calvary, a pen, and notebook.

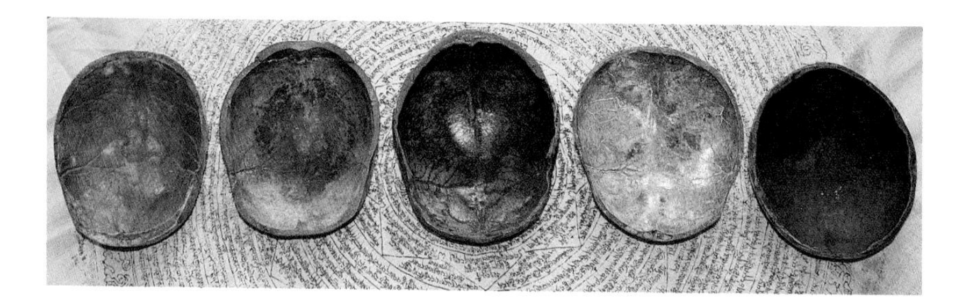

Tantric Carving said to depict and Alien

ARRIVING IN LHASA, TIBET

Not long after my meditation I felt myself flying through space. The scene that came into view was in bright technicolour; it was amazing. I was in the Himalayas, descending until I found myself sitting opposite a Monk, a Tibetan Monk. I was sitting on a very low beautifully painted bench. We were looking at each other across a low work table, the top was covered with smudges of coloured paint. He looked at me and smiled, as though he had been expecting me.

Potala Palace

Tibetans burning offerings outside Monastery

CHAPTER 3

IN THE PRESENCE OF ALIEN MONK

The Monk opened a conversation by explaining to me that although he was 120 years old, his face gave him the appearance of a thirty year old, which resulted in everyone calling him, the Alien Monk, but his real name is Sun Lin. He went on to tell me that his studio was his paradise, situated just a short distance from a Monastery, and his village, but he rarely visited either. His days were filled with painting Mandalas, using his own pigments made from crushed sapphires, coral, pure gold, and many other natural materials. Some of his Mandalas were bordered with precious and semi precious stones. The mud walls of his studio were covered with beautiful paintings. All the pictures are small to medium in size, with barely a hand space between them.

As I turned my head to look towards the window, Sun Lin pointed out that we were in the Himalayas, and he believed that there is no place on earth where he would find such peace in which to carry on the painting that had become his life. I turned my head back to look at Sun Lin. We looked at each other briefly in silence, but with a feeling of mutual trust and confidence.

Sun Lin explained that he had been painting Mandalas for more years that he could remember, striving to reach perfection in his work. The perfection that the Christian God reveals to us every day in this world, above, below, and all around.

Mandala painted using crushed precious and semi-precious stones

Leaving the Tibetan Monastery

When I was resident in the Monastery, I painted a Mandala every day, but the senior Monks took and sold my paintings even before they were dry. I was very upset because my work was lost to me forever, so too was the money the Monks were paid for my work. I asked Sun Lin if that was the only reason he had obviously left the Monastery. Not entirely. One of my reasons was that I was unable to communicate with the younger Monks, probably because half of them are children in training, a practice that is losing favour across Tibet, but my main reason for leaving the Monastery runs much deeper.

In the beginning I launched myself into the idea of becoming the highest achieving Monk in the Monastery. I quickly got into the relentlessly long periods of meditation. This involved wiping the mind of desires, fears, hopes and wishes, and the images from the devil that stray into the mind from time to time. Concentrating on breathing and breath, to reach the happiness where there would be no yearning after material things, or the frustrations of unfulfilled ambitions. The frequent periods of chanting mantra, OM MANI PADME HUM, continuing until my head felt that it would burst.

During one of the sessions, I had a spiritual moment. In a flash, I realised that there are special people like us, who do not ask to be special, but possess the ability to see the future for the world and everything in it. You and I both know that the world is always changing, and some of the changes ahead will be very significant and damaging for mankind. In that moment in time I realised I was becoming a detached zombie, and losing my psychic abilities. My greatest fear of all was that of losing my ability to paint, a fear greater than I could bear. I left the Monastery and settled into this studio, which for me has become truly my paradise on earth. A move I have never had cause to regret, even for a moment.

Mandala representing Deities painted in miniature, using a single Yak hair on Yak skin

Penitant's Faith

Mandalas are in the realms of sacred art, and that is why I strive to achieve the most complex development in my work. Mandalas are both an artistic form, and an important meditative tool to achieve integration with the Cosmos. This was recognised by your famous parapsychologist in the West, Carl Jung, in developing a treating his patients. He recognised the Mandala as a true therapeutic device for concentrating the mind, and liberating the mind from harmful obsessions. On occasions, Jung would have his patients construct a Mandala from coloured sands, and at the end of the process, the patient destroyed the Mandala to symbolise ridding himself of all his problems. As you know, this is a form of Structuralism, where the Mandala becomes sacred consciousness brought out into a physical form, over which the patient becomes able to exercise absolute domination and control, the point at which the patient is cured of his or her illness.

Dreaming of Aliens

Sun Lin spent hours sitting crossed legged on a low beautifully painted bench, just about two meters in length, staring at the Mandalas he had recently completed. I pointed out to him that some of his Mandalas featured beings from another planet. I asked him how he knew what an alien would look like. He explained that although he was told that he was born in the village, the villagers held that because of his great knowledge, wisdom, and his boyish appearance, he must be descended from aliens. I know that their ideas are nonsense, but they are probably responsible for my dreaming constantly about aliens. The aliens in my paintings are painted from the figures I see in my dreams. In my dreams, aliens arrive without warning in a craft that stirs up a great wind. Then of a sudden, as if a miracle, the craft with a skin that looks shell-like slowly becomes visible. Visible one minute, and gone as quickly as it came. In my dreams I sometimes opened the door to my studio, only to be blinded by a very bright light, after which I remember nothing until I found myself sitting on my bench in my studio, staring at my paintings. On occasions aliens spoke to me to explain

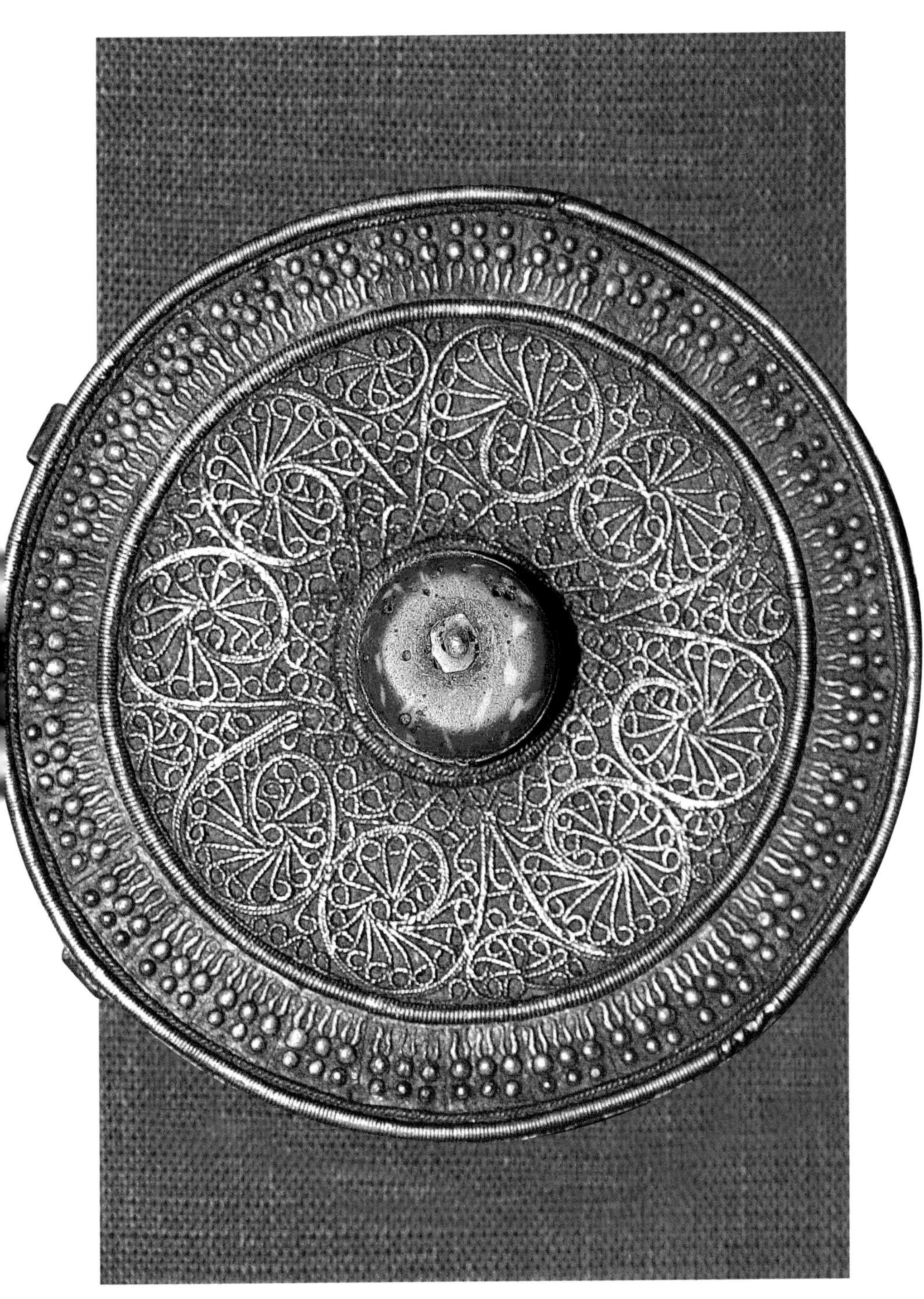

that the thin air in the Himalayas was comfortable for them, because it was the same as that on the planet from which they had come. Their long journeys posed no problems because the skin of their craft was self repairing under all circumstances. Contrary to the beliefs of our scientists, they travelled below the speed of light to avoid massive doses of radiation that would kill them. They told me that they had replaced my personal Ghau, with one they had modified to reveal to me the planet from whence they had travelled. The Ghau had at its centre a large red coral representing the sun, always their main reference point. Woven in delicate silver wire on the face of the Ghau were the trajectories to constellations from our planet. The smallest constellation at the edge of the Ghau represented their home planet trajectory.

The only model of a man of which I am aware that demonstrates our place on this planet Ronald, is Nostradamus, the greatest mystic of all time. He is alive in me, and alive in you, as I shall explain later.

Far back in history Ronald, Nostradamus foresaw the heat of the Sun on the Mediterranean destroying the marine life, and the staple food and luxuries to which the peoples around that sea have become accustomed, a scenario that will transmit around the world. You touch on some of his important work in your own book.

I know Sun Lin that we are living through the greatest age of scientific discovery the world has ever known. But I have also seen that our world will go through perpetual troublesome changes far into future time. Earth has a guardian planet in the planet Jupiter. This planet takes all the massive meteor strikes that are heading to planet Earth. Soaking up hits from meteors that would otherwise wipe out all life on planet Earth. Aside from the planet Jupiter, scientists feel that there is nothing to protect planet Earth from the ravages of mankind. They are mistaken. Our planet is a living cell, described accurately by that brilliant man Professor James Lovelock.

I believe Gaia will strike back by ridding the planet of the majority of human kind with earthquakes, massive volcanic eruptions, a scorching sun flooding, and scarcity of drinking water. These scenarios have just not arrived yet.

Disaster Looming Large for Himalayan Glaciers

Our neighbour Nepal, is beginning to see the dramatic effects of climate change. The rainfall is becoming unpredictable. Temperatures are rising. Mountain glaciers are melting into the lakes, and these will eventually burst their banks and destroy villages downstream. The loss of glaciers will deprive millions of people of drinking water. There is nothing positive that I can see on the horizon, and beyond.

There are more glaciers in the Himalayas than in all the polar regions. Glaciers that are the source of the River Ganges are shrinking at an alarming rate, and could be gone within the next fifteen years. The water from Ganga reaches down eventually to the flood plains that supply India's wheat and cotton crops.

The Flow of a Polluted Ganges Will Cease

By 2030 the Indian population will grow to one and a half billions, overtaking the population of China. This growth is fuelling environment disasters by increasing sewage and toxic waste flowing into the Ganges below every main village, on its way down to the flood plains. However, the water is so polluted the fish have already become poisoned where the river passes villages and town through which the waters flow on its way to supply four hundred million people in the Shanghai region. The Ganges supports ten per cent of the world population. Loss of glaciers supplying the Ganges, will only concentrate the pollution and poison in the water. The higher temperatures driving the loss of glacier ice is storing up a disaster for two billion people. Ice has continued to melt for the past one hundred years, but in two years the Himalayan ice will have melted below the fifty per cent tipping point, short of a sudden cold period that has arrived in the Northern Hemisphere, the lack of drinking water and running water will create an ecological disaster for India, Pakistan, China, Burma and others. Flooding in Bangladesh from the ice melt will cause havoc. In two years people living in these countries will be fighting over clean drinking water. When the problem becomes acute, India, Pakistan and China will explode into a war that only China can win. India and Pakistan will see it as fight or die. The problem building up will fetch a catastrophe beyond our comprehension. Wealthy developments such as Shanghai will be able to afford massive desalination plants to provide clean drinking water, but this will come at a cost, a cost that will be most probably unaffordable for the poor majority.

Most scientists on the planet Ronald, are preoccupied with the search through history for the clues to what made us what we are today. This is the easy way of scientific study. You are the only mystic with whom I have conversed, who is searching for what we will become in the future. A search for answers that is more urgent, and more important now, than at any time in human history.

Life on Earth will Change Beyond Recognition

Computerised virtual brains will constantly work on problem solving, and discovering new ways of doing everything. Most of mankind as a manual work unit will become obsolete by the millions, replaced by technology, new ways of doing, making, communicating and so on until this earth we know will be changed beyond belief. Science will create a new more advanced biological life. Superior human life will be created by scientists extending the human genome. Almost everything we were taught, know and understand from the past, will be turned on its head. Including the gathering and storing of energy, food production and methods of transport. All coming together to bring a new world for those who survive the calamities ahead. However, what science will never be able to do is to manufacture water from nothing.

I thanked him for his insight and knowledge. I told Sun Lin that what I would like is to discuss with him is that which I have seen lying ahead for the world; much of which I find very alarming. However, before we arrive at that subject Sun Li please explain to me what you see as the main differences between the Buddhist religion, and the mainstream religions of the west. First Ronald, I must tell you what life was like for Monks in the Monastery, bearing in mind that there are two and a half million Tibetans who follow the Tibetan beliefs.

SHEKAGARI

The Crystal Clear Mountain
Hides in the sunlight
And disappears into the night sky.

The butter lamps glow
And the demon traps
Shine in the darkness.
Mysterious and magical.

The boy does not see this.
Only the joy of the night travel.
As in a mirage the Monastery appears.

Pledged to Monkhood.
The horns greet him.
The ritual begins.
And the heart of the child
Speeds to the vibration of the soft chanting.

Lulled to sleep
The Monks gently carry him away.
The peace of the mountain
Dissolves him and brings him to paradise.

His mouth whispers softly as in a dream.
Tell them I am Shekagari.
This is the first day of my Life.

Sylvia Rayner.

CHAPTER 4

REALITY OF LIFE IN A MONASTERY

During my residency in the local Monastery, many monks confessed to me that they were not enjoying their arduous daily routine. Many young monks from the more wealthy families in Tibet, likened there day to a grim daily existence of self punishment. Certainly not the state of constant peace and happiness they were promised by their families, before their arrival at the reality of life in a Monastery.

Many monks used a string of beads as a way of gaining concentration for prayer or chant. We were told that a hundred beads moved were equal to around forty minutes of chanting. The monks sit in rows in the Lotus position. That is crossed legged with feet in the thighs, soles of the feet upwards. The back is held upright to enable the body to keep balance. Each session starts with chanting; then slowly closing eyes to encourage a meditative state, listening initially to the sounds all around. Breathing is allowed to continue as it wills. Minds move towards only a basic awareness of sounds all around by concentrating on the chanting. It is my opinion that self hypnosis then takes over normal consciousness. It has always been a source of amazement to me that states of consciousness can be transformed by mere chanting alone. The hypnotised condition is very real, and enables mind to reach a higher cognitive state.

Sun Lin continued; over the years since I left the Monastery, my opinion about the usefulness of the whole process and system has changed dramatically. People in the village are living in abject poverty, and depravation, at every level. Perhaps these young monks would serve a better purpose to the greater good if, instead of sitting chanting in the Monastery, they were creating more terraces for growing food, and learning the trades that would enable them to improve the housing of the poorest people living in this vicinity.

色拉寺辩经场
Debating courtyard

Monks debating a Koan
A Koan is a problem or riddle that admits no logical solution.

It is my opinion Ronald, monks travelling around the villager with their begging bowls; have become a burden on the villagers, taking from those who are working and struggling to feed their families, taking from people who do not have sufficient rice for their own needs. It is my dream that when the age of enlightenment comes to Tibet, it will be the monks who will be taking much needed food they have grown themselves out into the villages to feed the elderly, the infirmed, and the poor.

I have learned that I do not need any kind of ritual to awaken my soul to appreciating the beauty that is all around. In these mountains we see the glorious sun rise in the mornings, and spectacular sun sets at the end of the day, displaying beautiful rose pinks and mauve colours, that I endeavour to remember and for use in my paintings. Each night we look up at the stars above us, with the Milky Way glowing like a neon light. Everything in the sky moving relentlessly in a circle, proving to us that time passes away, a fate from which there is no escape for anyone.

OUR DAY BEGINS

As the Sun rises a new day dawns
And our whole being awakes
To the familiar sounds.
We are alive!
We have joy in our hearts.
Our day begins.

Remember what I told you
Purity of mind and spirit.
Love will grow from this.
And once again we will reach
The stars, where the Cosmos awaits us.

Think of the sheer pleasure of being here.
The human race, full of mystery.
A joy to see.
We have travelled far my friend.
When will our journey end?

Many will be left behind.
Many will be blinded
With no peace in their hearts
Only selfish thoughts
And no one to translate them.

Poor things, they will not listen.
They know they live
But for what reason?

They are already dead.

Sylvia Rayner.

Example of elaborate decorations in Monasteries

Nomadic Women collecting water from a Monastery Courtyard

ORA ET LABORA
PRAY AND WORK

Yes, you may see a Monk
Destined to prayer and poverty.
But this is not so my Friend.

As in a dream
The Sun will rise and the Sun will set
Leaving mankind to gaze in awe
And gather strength from this majestic sight.

At night I float into deep space, Gently soothed
As I sleep on a bed of Stars
My Magic Carpet to the edge of Time.
The Oracle awakes, And soon I drift back to the past
To the Shrine of God.

It is written in the Prophecy
Nothing must change. We are the future.
Life is that precious gift we all have.
It is our destiny.

So think well my friend.
What will you do with
This precious Gift?

I look at the stars each night.
And wonder. But joy overtakes me
And once more I am on the edge
Of the Universe.
I am free.

Sylvia Rayner.

CHAPTER 5
TRUTH ABOUT LIFE IN A TIBETAN VILLAGE

In my opinion Ronald, provinces or countries where Buddhism holds sway have need of strong government, because Buddhism is a way of life within a belief system. This is not the same as having a purposeful society developed from a framework of laws, as in the West. Until the intervention of China, Tibet remained an ancient feudal state captured and held in the past. A society doomed into drifting for centuries with one of the highest child mortality rates, no proper health system for the general population to speak of, and nothing in the way of a properly structured educational system for the population as a whole.

Please accompany me around the village Ronald, and see for yourself the pockets of how it used to be. What the Tibetan beliefs have not suffered from are the terrible atrocities of the West, when men women and children were tortured, and many burnt to death by the Catholic Inquisition on the orders of the Catholic Pope. Torture and murder that continued for hundreds of years, meted out to those who would not renounce their own religion and convert to Catholicism. Even in England hundreds of people were burnt to death at the stake on the orders of a Catholic Queen.

Strolling around the village Ronald, you will witness that Tibetan villagers have been conditioned by Buddhism to be content with their way of life, their lot, and prepare for happiness in their next life. The younger people, however, are quite different. Youngsters have become more confident than they were in the past, and more independent, but they nevertheless remain cautious, and conservative.

I found myself wandering around the village alongside Sun Lin, although no one appeared to notice my presence, which is a fascinating concept for another time. Sun Lin insisted on calling me Prophet, and gave me a

Yak Skin Bellows, Yak Tail Brush, Fire Striker

detailed commentary as we strolled along at a leisurely pace. The air is cold, and everyone is too busy surviving each day to pay us any attention, said Sun Lin. As you see Ronald, many of the homes are almost stone-age in appearance, and very crowded, with none of the proper facilities that are an essential requirement in almost every home in the West.

The Reality of Living in a Tibetan Village

I spotted an old lady, with a face like a dried prune, in a small dilapidated stone building standing in front of a black stove. She took a striker from a tinder box, using the striker to fire small pieces of yak dung laid in a circle. As the pieces came alight she threw them into the front of the black stove. She then prised a large round piece of yak dung stuck to the outside wall, broke it in two, and threw the two pieces into the stove. Filthy black dense acrid smoke issued from the tubular chimney, to which she appeared to be impervious. Not satisfied with the progress of the flames in the burner, she grabbed what looked like bellows made from yak skin with the long hair still attached, pumping it under her arm while directing a long thin nozzle into the fire. The whole thing looked like a 'Heath Robinson' contraption, clearly essential to her daily survival.

We stood watching in amazement at the process of lighting her boiler, then we looked down at a make shift table on the path, covered with leather belts decorated with white shells, and small brass bells, fluorite crystal, a small quartz crystal carving, and rose crystal. All the items were for sale at the price of ten Chinese Yuan, or ten pence, in English money. To my amazement, tied to the table with a piece of leather thong, was a small silver candlestick with a London Hallmark in the time of Queen Victoria. A man dressed like a nomad, came up to the table, paused and swung a fully packed yak backpack onto the stone path, calling out to the woman that all his goods were available for five Yuan. She came to his bag, peered inside and what appeared to be an argument ensued. We decided to move on.

Ancient Nomadic Smoking Kit

Nomadic Hunting Kit encompassing every conceivable aid for Surviving in the Mountains.

Tibetan Clay Yak Butter Teapot
with other items for sale

Tibetan Snow Leopard embossed in Copper

Painting of Deities on Yak Bone

Further along the path we passed a young Tibetan woman swinging her Prayer Wheel, before crossing to the opposite path, using her free hand to turn even larger prayer wheels set along the footpath. The atmosphere was destroyed for me when she sat on a sack and pulled out her mobile phone.

The spell broken Sun Lin turned to me to explain that winters in Tibet are very harsh. Many locals leave the territory to stay with relatives in warmer climes. We passed three small children with red rosy cheeks, wearing what looked like cosy and warm yak skin tops, gesturing with their hands to their mouths that they were hungry. Sun Lin explained that their rosy cheeks were not from good health, but their daily exposure to the suns deadly rays.

I will be staying in Tibet throughout winter to carry on with my work. Also to enjoy the warm and friendly gentility of my neighbours, who take their enjoyment from all the small things in life. We wait for Springtime to see the plants and flowers flourish in the sun, and the vultures circling overhead, looking to feast on the dead the monks carry up into the mountains on their back for a 'Sky Funeral'.

When we arrived back to the Studio, Sun Lin went to the stove in the corner, took a striker that was hanging from his belt, and lit a small amount of yak dung, threw it into the stove, and placed some pieces of coal from a basket onto the flames. Fortunately the tubular chimney from the stove went through the ceiling of his studio, and was a tight fit. I would not be choking today.

We sat opposite each other on the benches. Sun Lin opened the conversation. The moral concepts in the Tibetan beliefs are very strange. Some of these women are married to three, sometimes four men, usually brothers, all sharing one wife. Even stranger still, it appears to work for

3DNOV

them. It is sad but true that one in three children born to these women do not survive. The intense cold in winter and lack of proper food causes people to be very ill, in spite of fires fuelled by Yak dung burning day and night. The idea of one wife having several husbands comes down from the history of mysterious Mustang, above Nepal, where the queen was married to three husbands. This is a medieval land, where men and women eat the same food but prepared differently. The history of the place abounded with spirits that prowled, especially during the hours of darkness, when no person felt safe.

The Tibetan system does not allow young females to choose who they will marry, and this system is not uncommon in many other Asian countries. Future husbands for many Tibetan young girls are chosen by parents with the help of their local Shaman.

Tibet is around twice the size of the European Union, and yet only one percent of the land is used for agriculture, far too small an area to provide sufficient food for a growing population. Added to which there are problems created by the unpredictability of rainfall, which may amount to only a few inches in a year.

Every year many monks leave their Monasteries to return to their homes to help with the harvest. Winter is a bad time, because at this altitude there is only half the oxygen that will be found at sea level. Furthermore, tourists are scarce in winter, which results in there being very little work. Much of the rest of the year is dominated by agricultural life. Around this any spare time is dominated by Monasteries organising the local population to follow Tibetan rituals that have to be observed, the main and most important ritual being the celebration of the New Year.

Nomad Friends

Under the feudal system, before the Chinese took control, Tibetan Shamanism was a very big business. A good earner for the Shaman involved. Nowadays, the people realise that their pretend Shaman power to bring rain, are just another delusion, imaginary; as fanciful as their supposed healing powers, the casting out of spirits etc, all a nonsense. Many tourists who arrive in these parts are shocked by the poverty, and lack of hygiene in the villages, due to a shortage of water.

Ancient Shaman Mask

CHAPTER 6
Religion is Hardwired into the Human Mind

Why Sun Lin do Tibetan families send their young men to the Monasteries of Tibet. Many young men are pledged by their families to Monkhood, at thc age of ten years. This should not come as a surprise to you Ronald. There is a human need for religion or a belief system, by the peoples of all the countries on the planet. The reason is that the mind of human kind has an inbuilt process that grew with evolution of man, a process in the brain that is constantly looking for structure, and order, as part of the survival instinct, that is also part of the reasoning process going on in the mind; part of the blue print of the human brain. Mans very survival depends on the mind asking what is out there, what is all around us. The more uncertain the answers become, the more the mind turns to religious and supernatural structures for help. Evolution has ensured that everyone is captured by a natural instinct that seeks religion and the supernatural.

Holy Spirit Evolved as Part of the Evolution of the Human Mind

The human mind looks at God as a sacred supernatural power. A supernatural power that will keep a constant watch over mankind. A power that will tell us what to do in times of crisis, danger, or stress. When the mind evolved these beliefs, it felt secure in having found its place in the world; a meaning and a purpose. The mind of early man recognised that empathy was a tool for driving survival. This concept also evolved in the instincts of the animal kingdom. After this point in mans evolution the mind developed the Holy Spirit as a means of communicating with the power of the universe, that is a receptor of subtle powers permeating the universe. Holy Spirit had arrived, nothing to do with whether there is or is not a creator, but surrounded by subtle requirements for that receiver to switch on. With the unfortunate implication that as easily as the receiver can be switched on, unfortunately, it can be just as easily switched off.

The Teachings of Buddhism and the Western Church Fail All the Tests of Investigation

In the Tibetan belief system, some monks enjoy chanting together, and they have power and control over themselves. In the West, congregations in churches also enjoy singing hymns, or chanting prayer. All of which usually has the effect of making people feel good inside. In the West, however, the leaders of the principle religions have modified original scriptures to give themselves power and control by collective manipulation. One church in particular, forcing compliance and obedience to the Priesthood through ensuring their congregations obey collective group disciplines. Only then do priests promise that after resisting natural urges, and obeying group discipline, could church goers be raised to virtue and goodness. However, all of this only ensured that religion became a grim penitential life accompanied with a constant feeling of guilt and shame, and the ever present threat of divine punishment. In your country, church attendance is down to less than one percent of the total population, and the church leaders still pretend that this is not proof of abject failure. This decline will continue until church leaders wake up to and acknowledge the latest discoveries in science, archaeology, and original religious texts; rid themselves of pomposity, robes, crosses, and pretending supernatural happenings that break all the laws of the universe are real. Continue as they are going, without growing up, and they will fall to being regarded as an old superstition, much as is happening to the Tibetan belief system in these modern times.

Om Mani Padme Hum

Every trained monk in Tibet, chants the four word prayer, "OM MANI PADME HUM" which translates as 'The jewel in the Lotus', believing that there is hidden power in sound vibration. Most monks fix their gaze on a Mantra, trusting that it will increase the intensity of vibrations. They hope that by endlessly repeating this prayer, they will escape the cycle of birth and death, by going straight to paradise. Some monks believe that chanting is part of universal harmony, such as the harmony of the atom.

Scientists in the West have discovered Sun Lin, that memory retention of a scene without accompanying music reaches only forty five percent. Play music while gazing at a picture, and the memory retention of that picture is increased to ninety percent. My own opinion remains that chanting is part of the process of self hypnosis. There are however benefits to monks from these periods of self hypnosis such as the eradication of anxiety and tension.

Monks attribute all manner of mysticism and magic to Buddhist deities. None of which would stand up to investigation. History teaches us that Buddhist beliefs grew up in Pakistan and travelled to Tibet. It was these beliefs that shaped Tibetan Buddhism, except for the 'Book of the Dead'. However, in my view, consciousness of God in its simplest form needs no Monastery, Church, or organised priesthood.

Transendentalism and Mysticism are in Reach of Everyone

Literally anyone can embark upon the path of spiritual learning, or experience intense spirituality. No unorthodox or eccentric paths to spirituality are excluded from entering the realms of spirituality, mysticism or the contemplative. Nor is there a restriction to any particular age group. Muslim, Jewish and Christian mystics all search after union with the Transcendental or Devine. Contemplation of mystical should be focused on union with the Devine, until mysticism and the Devine become one. Following renunciation of oneself, as an entity separate from God, personality and consciousness of God merge. Unhappiness or despair fall away, and light begins to glow, in even the darkest of tunnels. An awareness of just being alive becomes so strong, everything else pales into insignificance. Meditation and prayer cost nothing, but they are the safest port in life's storms.

CHAPTER 7

TIBETAN BOOK OF THE DEAD

One of the teachings that took up much time in the Monastery, was the understanding of the 'Tibetan Book of the Dead'. A twelve hundred year old text that was written before Tibet converted from a military empire to Buddhism. However, pure Buddhism emerged originally two thousand five hundred years ago, when meditation was regarded in Asia as a simple method of centring one's life.

The Tibetan Book of the Dead was written in the eighth century, but is said to have remained hidden for six hundred years, when a devout Monk discovered the text in a rock pile beside the road on which he was travelling. Tibetan Monasteries commonly refer to his book as, 'The Bardo'. The writings are said to senior monks to reveal great treasures of philosophy, wisdom and enlightenment. The Bardo, is said to be a guide through the perils encountered travelling through the afterlife, direct to Paradise.

Ones deeds of good or evil before death will be paid for in this afterlife. For those who can afford it, monks chant for days, even weeks, beside the body, to ensure that the departed spirit will meet only peaceful deities, and not the blood sucking wrathful deities that everyone fears, along the complex and judgemental pathways. But if the souls hear the monks chanting, the departed spirit can leave safely, and be reborn, as animal or human. A nice earner, for the monks. However, the whole process is so complex it would take too long to go into all the details. Suffice it to say that the book helps Buddhists to become comfortable with looking at death. It is strange, however, that if you ever in your lifetime become involved with rehabilitating drug addicts, and listen to their experiences of terrible dreams, the thought forms they encounter in those dreams, are almost identical to those described in the Tibetan Book of the Dead.

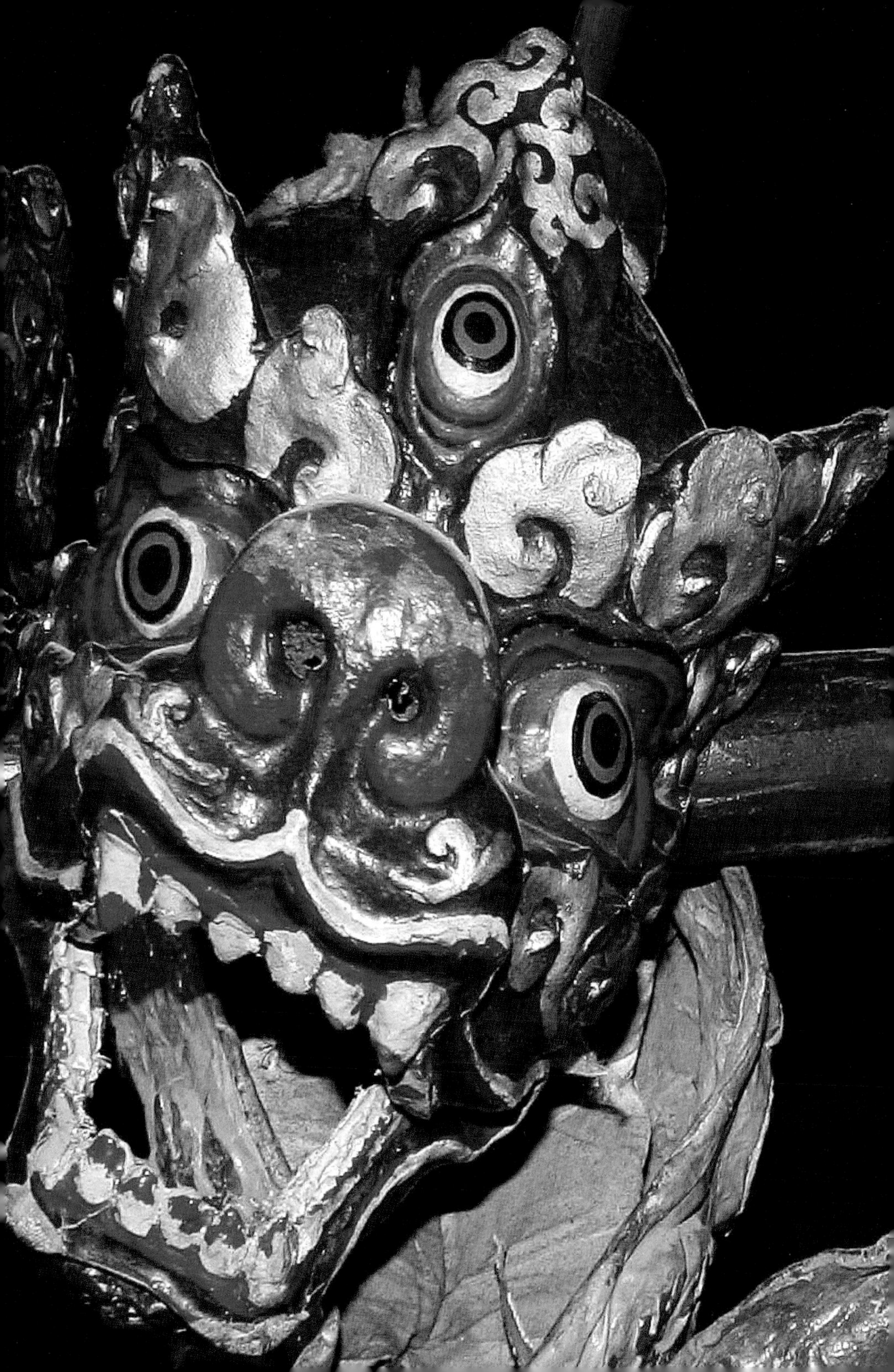

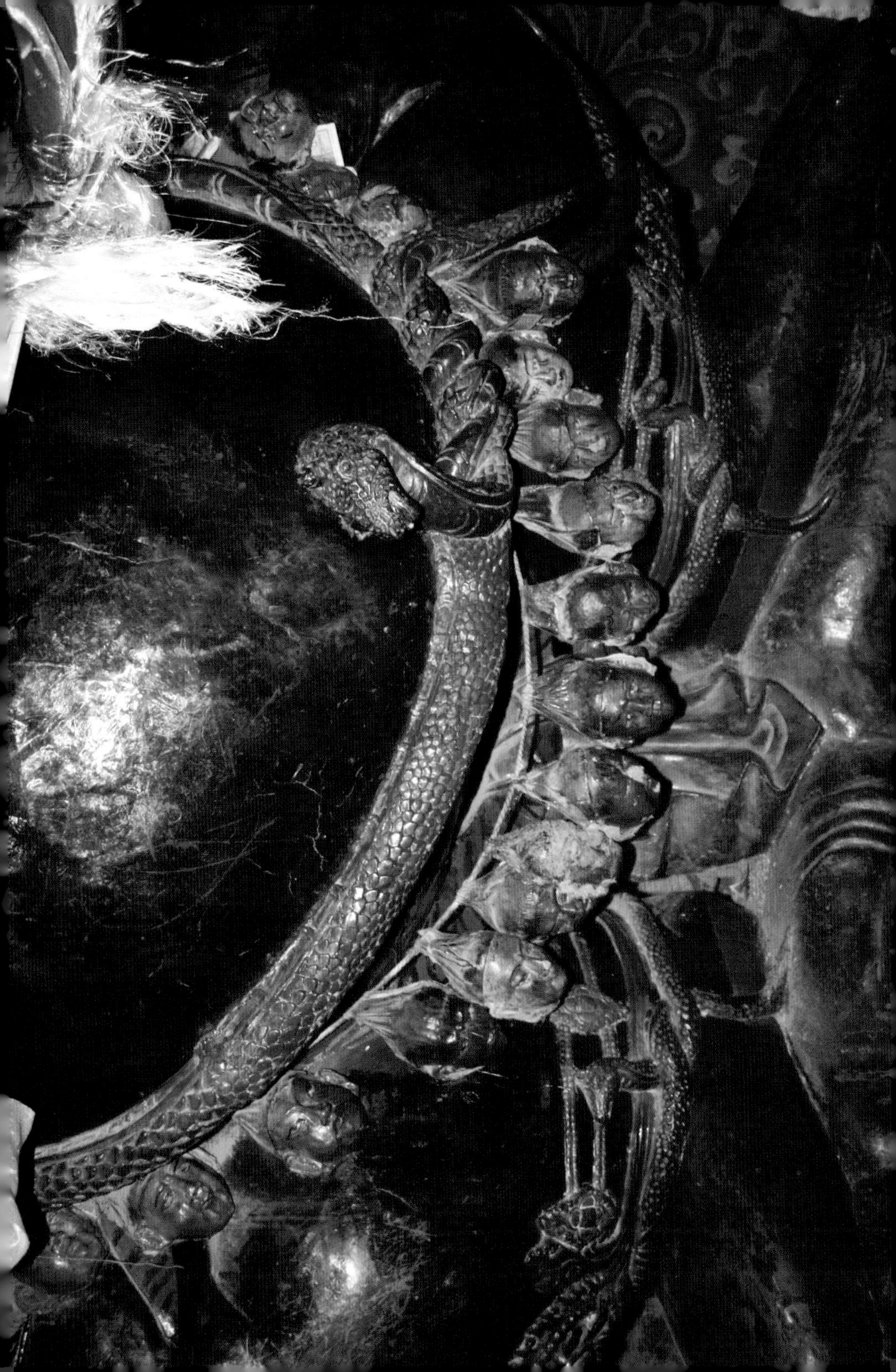

YI JIAO

Only Christianity is an Eternal Truth

One of my practices, said Sun Lin, that constantly annoyed senior monks at the Monastery, was for them to catch me studying the writings in the Old Testament, and other writings about Mysticism. They could not accept my response that when we looked out from the Monastery, we always see two things; the world before us, and the world as we see it, plus our feelings and ideas about that world before us. In the same way, religion and mysticism exist together, side by side, and it is chanting and self hypnosis that unlock the door to mysticism. The angry and intolerant response from the monks was just another reason that persuaded me that I no longer fitted in, and the right action to take was to leave.

A Vision Reveals the Eternal Truth of the Ten Commandments

What will interest you Ronald, is that my study of the Old Testament, the Commandments, the understanding of repentance; it was revealed to me in a vision, that Christianity is the only true religion in the world today. It was the Old Testament, and the Commandments, the beacons of justice, the point at which God instructed man to say NO to his worst thought, that shaped and formed the basis on which the whole of the Western civilisation grew, and its laws were laid out inside a solid framework in which people should lead their lives. The moral DNA to man, and those who allowed this embryonic fluid to flow over them and shape their lives, were rewarded by receiving Holy Spirit and Eternal Life. The Commandments also incorporated the beacons of justice, and the laws responsible for the civilising of the West. This vision was another reason that actually compelled me to leave the Monastery.

I understood that when the Prophet Moses went up to the Mountain to receive the Commandments, it was the greatest happening in the whole of human history, and the first unequivocal example of Mysticism on planet earth. After which came the development of science, but it is important that the two should not be confused, although there are occasions when interconnectedness between them is revealed. All very different to our part of the globe where there are many religions and many Gods, none of which can stand up to any investigation looking for eternal truth.

NOW CAN YOU SEE?

Take my hand Nostradamus
My dear friend.
Breath slowly and gently.
I will take you to the hidden land.
There you will see the cruelness of mankind.
The selfish future etched from sin.

No kindness, no love
No joy, no self esteem.
Only selfish squalor called money and greed.

Is there no end to this?

Envy, jealousy, eating at a Nation.
Nowhere to go but the future
Where death only awaits them.
Poor things, lost and forgotten.

A Pity.

Here in the mountains we find peace.
We worship the wonderment of nature.
Pureness of the spirit and soul.
Here we find love and trust.
Dedication, a purpose.
Here we find the truth.

Now Can You See?

Sylvia Rayner.

CHAPTER 8
MYSTICISM, SCIENCE, AND NOSTRADAMUS

You Ronald understand clearly how and why mysticism and science have both played separate but most important roles in the development of mankind; his society and community. You can see why science and mysticism co-joined to reveal ultimate truths. Nostradamus used both to develop his capacity as a Seer to project events in future time on to the parchment of his day. Your burden will be that while you have seen and understood this secret knowledge; how difficult is it be reconcile in your mind that no one else sees or knows the catastrophe that will flow around the planet in future time. The life of the Seer is one of being separate and different to those around you. This brings a feeling of being alone, and the loneliness that follows, buoyed up by the knowledge that no one is closer to God than a Seer and Prophet. We are few and we are rare. Nostradamus was the only true Seer on the planet in his time. It may be that you are the only true Seer on the planet in your time. Let it be so. I know that God has already put those in place those who will protect you, and will bring down those who plan against you.

You are probably the only person in the West who has cracked and understood the methods used by that great Seer Nostradamus, in making his predictions for events far into the future. One of the basic tenants of his work was his use of astrology. The use of astrology and its credibility, become obsolete some time after the death of Nostradamus. The French Academy of Science banned astrology in the seventeenth century, after which astrology left the main stream of science, only to survive as an entertainment, much as it does today. Although the practice of astrology is still taken very seriously in many Asian countries, and it is likely that Asians will want to hang on to anything that tells them what they want to hear. Good words should be listened to from whatever source they come, but the predictions by Nostradamus often fell well short in their timing and promise. Although this weakness in his work was often explained away by writers as the necessity to disguise his predictions from the prying eyes of the Catholic Priests, a prediction is either right, or it is wrong, and many if his were wrong. It does not take a man of genius to predict that earthquakes, volcanic eruptions, and meteor strikes lie ahead in the future. Predicting accurately why and when disasters will come upon the earth, is something more special.

Tibet Conclusion

No one should doubt that the chanting of prayers, the turning of personal and giant communal prayers wheels, has been transmitting out into the ether over Tibet, every minute of every day of every year, for centuries. And yet no discernable material benefits, benefits to health, or reduction in child mortality has accrued to the peoples of the Tibetan town and villages, in the form of any reward for their devotion and efforts over many lifetimes, following the Tibetan belief system.

As an independent analytical factual unbiased observer, I try to take something from every conversation or anything I observe. What I take from this conclusion is proof positive that the human mind is hardwired to reach out to some form of belief or belief system, where personal input or ritual will bring hope of personal good fortune and happiness in the future. A belief system that will prevail without any sign of reward, as long as someone with weasel words is in place to urge them on, and reward his leadership, with loyalty, money or goods.

CHAPTER 9

COUNTLESS MILLIONS WILL DIE WHEN THE GLACIERS MELT

Why is it so important Sun Lin, to know God at this time? I'll tell you Ronald, there are more dangers ahead for the survival of human kind that at any time in human history. There are also many dangers ahead for the survival of most of the species on planet earth.

Tell me Sun Lin, what great dangers or catastrophes do you see lying ahead that will come into effect in the next few years. Starting with our own Himalaya, Ronald, we have some three thousand kilometres of mountain, and many of the highest mountains in the world that are home to three thousand glaciers. These glaciers provide the rivers and drinking water for two billion people below the Himalaya. Some of these glaciers have lost more than half of their ice. If this meltdown due to global warming continues at its present rate, river flows in the next twenty years will slow to a trickle. The effect on China, India, and Pakistan, will be catastrophic, and may lead to war between China, India and Pakistan, on the basis of fight or die. The problem does not stop there. Not very far from the source of the flow of the river Ganges high in the mountains, the fish in many of the rivers lower down flowing through the towns, are now poisoned. Poison that is now entering the Pacific Ocean.

Time is Running Out for the Survival of Millions

The river flows on to Shanghai, where the water is already very polluted, due to the growing unprecedented levels of river traffic, and is set to worsen, because Shanghai is undertaking one of the largest construction projects in the world which will involve three hundred million people, more than the population of the whole of America, moving in from the countryside, where they have a small carbon footprint, and into the suburbs, where their carbon footprint will at least treble. As you see, there is no end in sight for the increase in carbon emissions in China. But judging by China's track record on solving difficult technical problems, there is probably no country in the world more capable of taking the problem in hand. However, it is very clear, that the end is in sight for many people in these regions.

One of the most fascinating predictions I have seen Ronald, is when you saw The Power of the Universe, whilst scrying with the 'Skull of Doom', in your book, 'Joseph Escapes to Glastonbury'. That experience adds even more catastrophes, than those of which I was aware.

The **Skull of Doom**

I sat in my chair in my garden, with the sun going down preparing to enter trance meditation holding the hand of Wilson the skeleton sitting next to me.

In my pocket was my piece of Calvary given to me by Sister Katerina who tended the Altar of Crucifixion in the Holy Sepulchre when I was filming my Documentary Jerusalem. I always held the piece of Calvary in my hand during my prayer for protection before scrying. Whilst I felt confident scrying with the Skull of Doom, I did not feel inclined to hold the skull during the proceedings. I decided to leave that pleasure to Wilson the skeleton who was wearing the Urim and Thummin, as worn by the High Priests when scrying in the Temple of Solomon. Inside the small pots on Wilsons Breastplate were real precious and semi precious stones, as used at the time. Wilson sat with us at the dining table during our afternoon strawberry tea, to set the mood of preparation.

What I saw during the scrying was in vivid technicolour and quite scary.

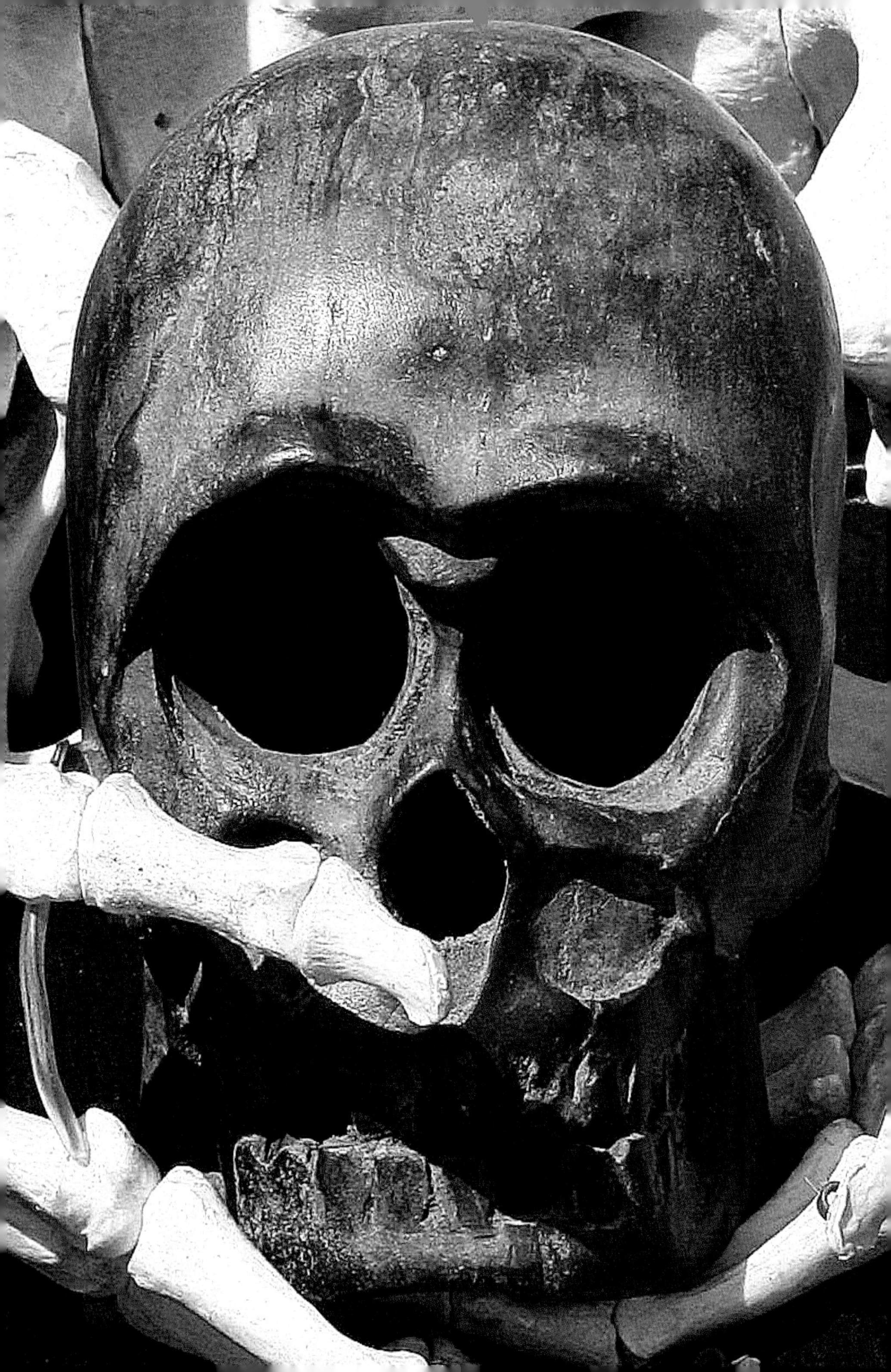

I Saw a Great Skeleton, Striding the Oceans, Calling to Me. My Waters are Warming My Prophet.

My Fish and My Creatures will Die. Great will be My Wrath, Upon Those who have Poisoned My Soul. I will Sack My Land. I will Return It to the Sea. I will Burn the Land. I will Burn the Forests. I will Flood the Coasts and Cities, until I have Washed Away the Poison. Poison will Rise from the Depths of My Oceans. There will be Wars with those Who Try to Escape My Wrath .Man will Destroy Himself and his Filthy Ways. Keep Watch on the Night of the High Tides. Do Not Sleep, Less you Perish in My Waters. Keep Watch when My Sun is Hot, Less you Perish in the Heat.

My Punishments are Coming. I will Passover Those I Love, and Those Who Love Me, and Keep My Commandments, or Repent Their Evil Ways, I will Not Take Away Their Time and Eternity. Others Who are Not of My Way, Shall Perish in My Waters, the Poisoned Air, or Burnt by My Sun.

My Earth Shall Not be, Entirely Destroyed by My Waters.

A Stone, Uncut by Human Hand, Shall Fall from the Heavens. A Great Mountain will Arise Upon the Earth. My Divine Punishment will Cease. A New Age will Begin.

I am convinced that the calamities that lie ahead for many countries will become very real, far sooner that people expect, but please explain to me Sun Lin; what are the major differences between Christianity and Buddhism that persuaded you to switch your faith from Buddhism to Christianity.

THE PRAYER WHEEL TURNS

Pouring water we baptized one another.
Then the mountain erupted
With heavenly chanting.
Sending me into a trance.
The banks of the Jordan once again
There to feel, touch and see.
I was that young Monk who knew Jesus.

These kind people bless me
And I accept their gift,
Their prayers beyond belief.
I join these beautiful people.
Jon Jon they cried.
We love you.
And so the prayers continued
Ever pouring out as an everlasting Mandala.

As the Holy Water passes my lips
I wonder at its journey.
Hundreds of years to reach me.
To nurture me.
Refresh me and cleanse me.
This simple substance the Elixia of Life.

I reach for my favourite Mandala.
It comes to life in my hands
And it too travels into space.
Around the Universe, to return once more
To my secret dwelling.

As the clock strikes.
The prayer wheels turn.
The messages on and on journeying
Into magical space.

Under my feet the Manu stones vibrate.
The white rags sending messages to the highest peak.
The vibrations soothing the traveller.

Drawn by the power of the mountain they follow.
Their path leads to enlightenment.
They are as one.
Om Manu Padme Hum.

Brothers and Sisters
God Bless You All.

Sylvia Rayner.

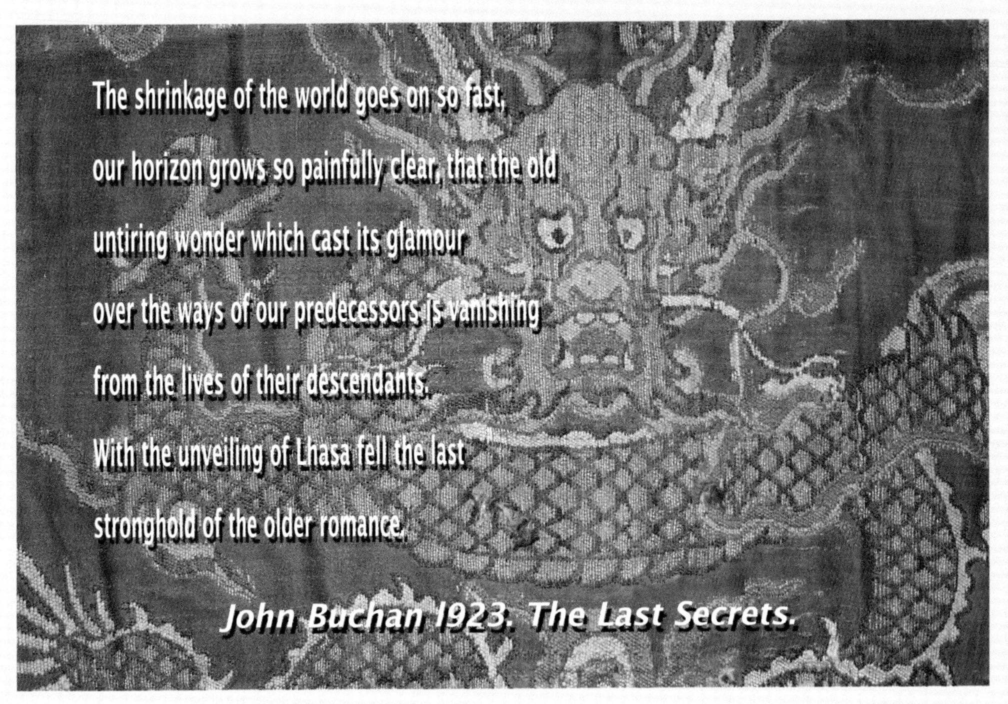

Buddhism does not Recognise God as the Devine Power of the Universe, or that the Holy Spirit is Direct from God

Tibetan Buddhism neither recognises, or acknowledges God, as the Divine Power in the Universe. Neither does Buddhism recognise the HOLY SPIRIT from God. I have spent most of my life pondering these questions Ronald, and the conclusion I have reached after long searching in my heart, is that Buddhism is a Belief System, with precepts that should be obeyed by monks that are obedient to the belief system, and is not a religion.

Buddhism requires its adherents to withdraw from society in search of the wisdom that will be attained by following the eight fold path; Right Belief, Right Thought, Right Speech, Right Action, Right Livelihood, Right Exertion, Right Self Discipline, Right Meditation. With the aim of ceasing all sin.

Buddhism does not have Baptism for Remission of Sins

What Buddhism does not have, however, that leaves it without the most important of all foundations, is Baptism. John the Baptist, cousin of that great Prophet Jesus, was the first true Monk in the world. John lived in the Wilderness of Judea, surviving on locusts and wild honey. He was the Son of Zachariah, a Temple Priest and Elizabeth, a cousin to the Blessed Virgin Mary. John was aware of the extraordinary happenings surrounding his birth. John lived in the Desert of Judea, to the southwest of Jerusalem. He lived along the banks of the Jordan. John demanded remission of sins and ablution in water to wipe away sin. This is just another of the basic fundamental principle around God that separates Buddhism and Christianity.

CHAPTER 10
SUCCESS IN CRACKING THE SYSTEM USED BY NOSTRADAMUS

I believe Ronald, that the reason you are here, and why we are enjoying these conversations, is that you and I understand the structure and the systems used by Nostradamus when he was making his predictions. What conclusions Ronald, about the man and his system of scrying to foretell future have you reached.

Well, Sun Lin, I believe that I know and understand precisely how Nostradamus achieved his results. First we must acknowledge our respect for Nostradamus, a man who was the greatest mystic in history, and whose predictions are as much talked about and written about today as they were in times past.

There was very little science available to Nostradamus in the sixteenth century, in which he lived. What was at his disposal was Astrology, and Scrying, and he used both of these tools extensively. We are aware that in the present day Astrology has been discredited, but in 1547 Nostradamus used the stars to apply dates to the results of his scrying. I do not doubt that what he predicted in his scrying was very real to him, but the dating of the events through his use of Astrology, are in my opinion, very unreliable on time scale. Bearing in mind that the task of calculating the progress of star patterns well into the future, without the aid of a computer in his day, should not be underestimated, albeit that the results could prove very inaccurate. Obviously Nostradamus felt his work was sound, because looking at first principles only, the progress of star patterns should not change, because Newton had proved that planets really did move, and I suspect that this confirmation from that great scientist set Nostradamus on the course he took outside his practice of medicine.

I do not doubt that in his scrying, Nostradamus saw that because planets did move, there could be no peace or harmony on earth.

Earthquakes, erupting volcanoes, storms and surges in the sea, a boiling Sun, freezing winters and nations railing and warring against each other with great cruelty and loss of life and limb are rather obvious, and could be foretold for the planet well into the future. The rhythms of the planet are fundamental. Something that cannot be changed, but instead of pointing the way ahead, a journey to the Garden of Eden, the progress of the star pattern foretold of unimaginable sufferings brought about in some cases by the actions of man himself, warring on others.

Nostradamus Constructed His Own Ephemeris Tables

His methods, were as simple as showing that when Mars, God of War, was ascendant over a certain period, to Nostradamus this event augured war on the planet earth itself. Nostradamus must have used tables he made himself to be able to discern the movements of the twelve signs of the Zodiac to be able to place likely dates for catastrophes to come about. But it was further necessary for him to enter into trance scrying, in the hope of seeing the detail surrounding the events. However, in order to avoid being tortured or burnt at the stake by the Catholics, his predictions would have to be concealed in a code Catholics would not understand. A local Catholic Priest once told me that God was with us always in our suffering, and suffered the pain that we suffered. Surely, I replied, if you believe what you say, you Catholics must have caused God to suffer every time you tortured men, women and children, in your prisons, who refused to renounce their beliefs during the Catholic Inquisitions.

CHAPTER 11

FUTURE TIME

GRIM OUTLOOK FOR MOST OF THE PLANET

We have now reached that time Ronald when we can speak together to discuss your new exciting scrying experience, using the same instruments as those used by Nostradamus. Tell me what has been revealed to you about the future for planet earth, and whether it is as serious as we both fear.

Confining my search to the Himalaya, USA and the Northern hemisphere, and a cursory look at Europe, Sun Lin, the outlook is grim, to the point that I would advise anyone thinking of moving to live in those climes for the longer term to consider very carefully before doing so. I would certainly advise anyone against taking up residence in India, Pakistan, China, or America. I advise them not to set up home and plan for children in those countries.

FIFTY YEARS OF ECONOMIC DECLINE FOR EUROPE AND USA NUCLEAR CONFLICT AHEAD FOR AMERICA

To begin with, I saw that the World Banking Crisis signalled the start of fifty years of economic decline for Europe and USA. As opposed of fifty years of economic upturn ahead for China, India, Brazil and Russia, brought to a premature halt for India and China by the calamities ahead triggered by global warming events, and sustained high birth rate in India.

The reasons for these unexpected astonishing changes ahead are staring everyone in the face. In China, and parts of the Indian continent, people will work enthusiastically for ten hours a day for just two US dollars or four Euros; without job security and any other benefits to which Europeans and

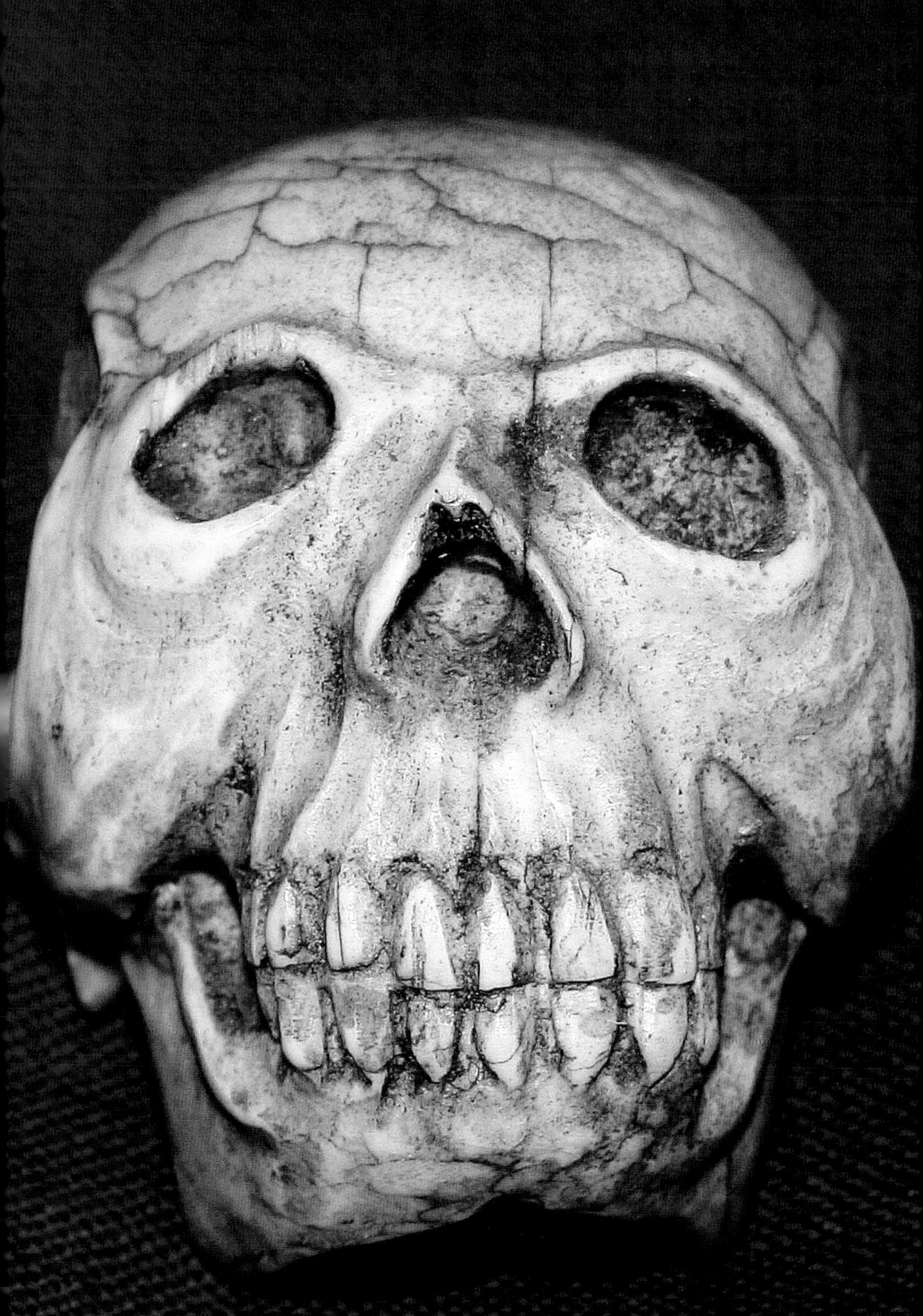

Skull found in cave by Craig Allen Rayner, said to be of Alien Origin.

Americans have become accustomed. As a result, China and India have by far the lowest production costs in the world. Added to which most of their costs for material are the lowest in the world. Compare this with the Western economies where the work ethic is for reduced working hours, and ever increasing pay, and longer holidays, to give more time for binge drinking and binge eating. Early retirement with the receipt of generous non contributory pensions, is enjoyed by many. Other employees of the State receive a full time salary, excessive holidays plus a generous pension, whose working hours actually on the job, amount to little more than part time employment. It is clear to see that many countries in the West are living in a fool's paradise that cannot be sustained, and will slowly collapse as more and more world calamities brought by global warming come upon them. US borrowings will continue at a rate that is so high lenders will realise US borrowings can never be repaid in a single lifetime The American economy and the value of the US dollar will begin to falter before entering into a slow continuous collapse.

Nuclear War in the Future

In my next scrying session I saw that the world is approaching a time of the antichrist, a time when major world economies will develop conflicts that will escalate into nuclear war. Two wars will arise in the Middle East, triggered by a strong unprecedented resurgence of Arab nationalism brought about by the following scenario;

Everyone knows that the free availability of oil is absolutely essential, and of fundamental importance to all major world economies. When the American troops leave Iraq, they will leave behind a legacy of well trained Iraqi troops and a well trained police force. After the Americans have left Iraqi soil, Iran and Syria will start to court Iraq in earnest. Iraq will gain the strength and confidence to build up an Arab bloc against the countries that invaded its soil. Other Arab oil producing nations will join a coalition of oil states and sign an accord to substantially increase oil prices on the grounds that their oil is running out. This new found strength and confidence will empower the Arabs to constantly turn the screw on oil supplies, driving up oil prices to unheard of levels, achieving their aim of harming the West.

War Over Oil Supplies

The West will sit watching helplessly as their economies collapse. The governments of the West will then raise an agenda for the invasion of those oil rich countries that are unnecessarily withholding oil supplies. The Arab response will be, "it is our oil, and we will sell it to whoever we choose and the price we choose to sell". The concerted response from the west will be a joint nuclear attack with small tactical nuclear weapons, in order to circumvent a drawn out conflict that would only exacerbate the world shortage of oil still further. Russia and China will decide to sit on the sidelines, knowing that the West, with the might of its combined military machine will win in the end.

Israel Attacks Arab Nations with Nuclear Weapons

Mixed in with this conflict, Iran, Syria and other Arab nations will come together to aid the Palestinian struggle against our Israeli friends. Israel will respond with a small but limited attack using small tactical nuclear weapons against Arab forces massing outside its borders. The world will be in a tumult and turmoil never before seen. America will ratchet up the pressure by attacking Northern Regions of Pakistan with small nuclear weapons, as a warning to other Arab nations that nothing is ruled out, including nuclear war on all fronts. Millions will feel desperate, helpless and suicidal.

Adding to these conflicts, world governments will fail to prevent people dying in their millions from the calamitous effects fetched by global warming, that will continue its pattern of periodic destruction by the heat of the sun, hurricanes, flooding, earthquakes, tsunamis, volcanic eruptions, starvation, and lack of drinking water.

You, my prophet Ronald, are a carbon copy of myself. We both live close to the world, but we do not live in it. This is why we alone are able to discern the events lying ahead in future time, and we have seen and recognised the shadows being cast forward by these events. We can both look around anything to observe it, and we, both of us are also capable of absorbing ourselves into that object, and we both know that certainty is born of mystical ability of insight.

We also draw in the right thoughts at the right pace inhabit those thoughts where mysticism arises during the intensity of depth of feelings. Seeking out the ultimate truths of the connections of those events in time, and perceive what is happening as a consequence of those processes. Then capturing, memorising, drawing on these moments which then begin to pull at us in the same way that beauty and truth pull at us.

CHAPTER 12

A Super Hurricane will Bring New York to a Standstill and Slows America's Growth

Tell me Ronald, what was the first catastrophe you saw to strike the continent of America. I tell you this Sun Lin, what I have seen gives me cause for concern, particularly when our history shows that it was the English genes flowing through the veins of the earliest civilised Americans that set the USA on the road to greatness. More particularly, George Washington, the first American President, who was descended from English stock, whose great, great, grandfather, was a Preacher in a local village, and whose remains are buried in a church in my local town, Maldon, in Essex, England. Even my own ancestry, which is traced back to 1066, contains the name of the first ever Clinton, gives me a natural affinity with our American cousins.

The first calamity I saw was a massive hurricane forming off the Caribbean turning right to track along the east coast of America. Winds in excess of two hundred miles an hour pushed the seas inland along the coastal areas, covering land with five meters of sea water; continuing along to sweep around the coast from Florida, up along the coastline until moving inland from Washington to New York, filling underground train tunnels completely. In New York, the inundation of water continued to rise until it was ten feet above the street level, bringing New York, and the whole of its financial district to a complete standstill.

America's Grain Crop Fails

In complete contrast, global warming brought a grim drought across Americas Southwest. Intense heat and lack of rain was drying up the Colorado River basin, and affecting the availability of clean drinking water for millions of Americans. Huge swathes of the Southwest were becoming affected by desertification. As time went on the Colorado River became little more than a trickle. Crops were failing in a big way over huge areas of farmland. Soil was literally turning to dust. Winds caused black blizzards across a million acres from Texas to Dakota. There appeared to be no end to the misery in sight all along a line from Colorado to Las Vegas, across to Phoenix. There was a mass movement of people towards North America where water was plentiful. The East coast of America revealed a story that was very different. All manner of changes were taking place in the North Atlantic that was having far reaching effects.

Huge Swathes of Farmland Blighted

The worst consequences from the American crop failures were being felt on the African continent where millions of people and farm animals were dying. That great nation, the USA, that feeds the poor of the world, was struggling to find sufficient grain for its own needs.

The blight on huge farming areas across the Americas brought chaos to Wall Street. There were huge swings in the world value of the US Dollar, as the American economy in general starts to falter. Lenders become reluctant to finance the massive US deficit. China turned away from America as a main buyer of US debt when it realised that America would be unable to help China with its own food shortages.

Tsunami Strikes from San Francisco to Vancouver

Looking to the west coast of the Americas, along the line from San Francisco to Vancouver, Canada, there was earthquake activity out to sea that looked to be fetching a Tsunami that would be striking the coastal areas.

Looking towards the Arctic, the sea ice in the summer had gone, but the rise in sea level predicted by scientists was not discernable. However, there was continuous volcanic activity off Iceland, and obvious disturbance in the mid Atlantic between Iceland and Canada. Two volcanoes were erupting on Iceland, one much larger and of greater strength. The debris was extending Iceland's coastline, and causing surges in melt water from a nearby glacier.

Arctic Conditions Prevail for the Northern Hemisphere

Looking back again at North America and Canada. The whole area was covered with arctic like conditions; low temperatures not experienced in the past. Ice storms, snow storms, and loss of power supplies brought the misery that goes with such events. This was not an exceptional condition. It will become the winter norm for North America and Canada. Conditions that are in stark contrast to those predicted by scientists.

Looking across to the United Kingdom, an unfortunate mixture of weather prevailed, as a result of the warm current flowing up from the Caribbean slowing by some thirty percent.

Some features were scary. In my previous books, I talked about the 'Rayner Line', an area under a line from just beyond the Isle of Wight, running at a roughly forty five degree angle to the 'Wash' in the Midlands. The area under this line becomes England's, Garden of Eden, and escapes all the worst excesses of the freak weather to come. I did not see any discernable rise in sea levels. What was alarming was the increase in frequency of hurricanes escaping from the Caribbean areas into the North Atlantic. These brought severe weather to Ireland, Wales and Scotland. The effect was that coastlines were battered by high seas and two hundred mile an hour winds.

Winter conditions for these areas looked even worse. Arctic weather was sweeping across Ireland and into the North of England; Wales, Scotland the north of England. Arctic blizzards brought everything to a standstill. Those Arctic spells were not long lasting but caused havoc for everyone.

These were conditions not seen for centuries. Power shortages in the UK only made matters worse. Many of the propeller driven wind towers set in place to provide electricity came tumbling down. The result was a permanent shortage of power for some areas of the UK. Parts of the sea on the North Sea coast froze over.

The West Midlands entered some calamitous weather, where on occasions four weeks of rain fell in a single day. Rivers were overflowing and merging into great floods, washing out power substations, water purification plants, factories, causing reservoirs to overflow. Animals drowned, crops were ruined. A new triangular lake appeared in the Midlands that would not go away. Everyday weather forecasts will appear to be normal, but these extreme events will come unannounced.

I noticed a massive Tsunami building up in the Mediterranean Sea, and heading towards Southern Italy, destroying much of the depleted fish in the Mediterranean, and causing massive damage on shore. Shortly after this disaster I saw a new phenomenon that looked like an earthquake storm, across the Bosporus, a straight between European and Asian Turkey, linking the Black Sea and the Sea of Marmara, spreading out into Italy and Greece, with disastrous widespread consequences.

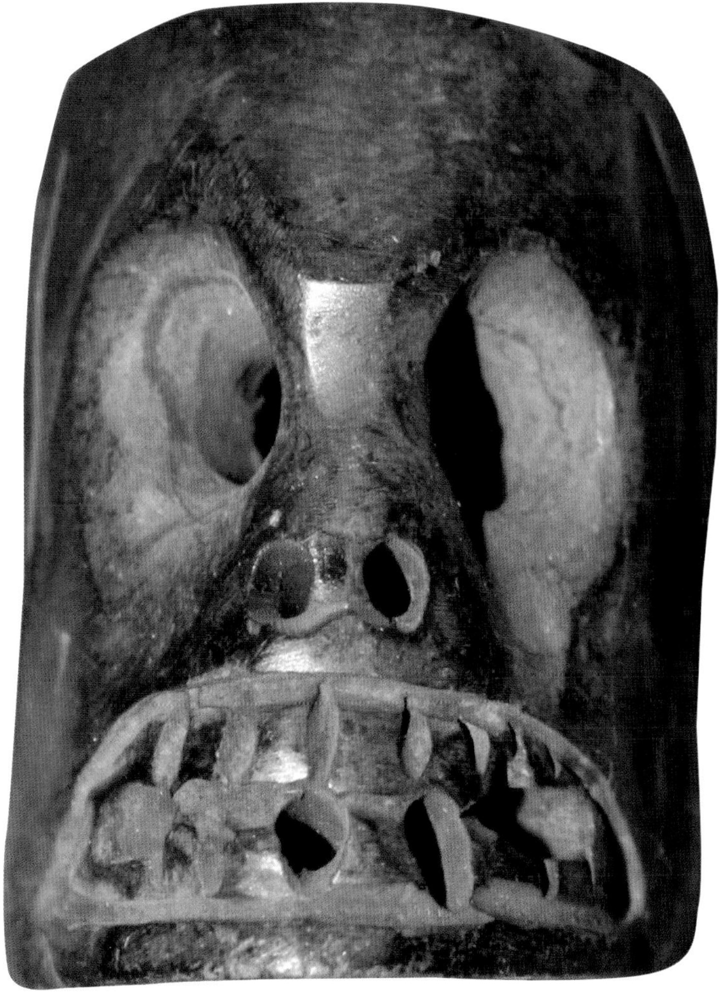

CHAPTER 13

TOKYO DISAPPEARS UNDER A MASSIVE EARTHQUAKE

I saw a massive earthquake under TOKYO, Japan. An earthquake, more serious than the Kobe quake, the consequences of which would have consequences for economies throughout the world; triggering the second world Banking Crisis. The earthquake felt as if it would continue forever. I looked up because the sky above Tokyo appeared to be on fire. Chemical tanks full of poison, oil and petrol in refineries exploded and raged into the upper atmosphere, before raining down upon people, and peeling their skin from their bodies. About half the buildings all around just disappeared into the ground, as did the people who lived in them; the result of liquefaction, when the ground becomes quicksand. Buildings that did not sink appeared remarkably undamaged, but there was no road or ground beneath, just a building atop its concrete piles, like something from a Salvador Dali painting. There were no people around, almost everyone was dead.

The following day news of the catastrophe spread around the globe sending Stock Markets around the world into free fall. When it became obvious to the Japanese Government that it would take many years to recover from such a massive disaster, world credit markets came to the realisation that the huge cash surpluses from Japanese trade with the rest of the world would no longer be available for many years. World credit developed a squeeze as high as the Empire State Building. This turmoil continued as the Japanese Government started to sell overseas Bonds to pay for the reconstruction of their Country. The earthquake proved to be the largest and most devastating in world history, giving birth to the second most serious World Banking Crisis in world history.

CHAPTER 14
APOCALYPSE RED TIDE FOLLOWS COLLAPSE OF FISH STOCKS

What Ronald, do you see as one of the major coming catastrophes already written in future time, from which the world will not recover, and which will endanger the survival of many people on earth. Sun Lin, I have seen the Biblical Red Tide of the Apocalypse. Scientists understand and know what the Red Tide is, but are not fully aware of all its causes. Red Tide is fatal to fish and other creatures in the seas, and can be fatal to human kind. This generation will witness, The Red Tide of the Apocalypse.

Allow me to start at the beginning. Huge high tech vessels from Japan will give fishermen directions to all the biggest shoals of fish around. Unbelievably large Japanese fish processing vessels will deal with, and store the fish, and the harvesting of fish spawn. These fleets and their fishing vessels are already emptying oceans around the world. Stocks of Alaska Herring and stocks of Blue Fin Tuna will collapse in the seas around the world, from which they will not recover. The fishing fleets will move on to take whatever remains in the seas, including the sea floor. Continuous heating of the oceans by the sun, poisons feeding into the oceans from polluted and poisoned rivers draining from landmasses around the world, will bring about the collapse of the greatest food source on the planet. Millions of people around the world will suffer malnutrition and slow starvation. The seas will never recover during this cycle of human kind.

Now follows the RED TIDE. Fish will be replaced in many areas by crustaceans, mostly the lobster species. It is the crustaceans that will release the overload of toxins that turn the sea red. The seas will empty, people will die, by which time the next Apocalypse will be on its way.

CHAPTER 15
PLANET EARTH TILTS TO A NEW HORIZON

I saw the build up of ice in the Antarctic continue. In complete contrast, all ice in the Arctic had completely melted in some areas enabling great vessels to sail across the top of the globe, moving through areas that had not previously been open to shipping. Areas of sea that had remained iced up for thousands of years.

Celebration of this new shipping route faltered, as the world noticed it was looking at a new horizon. Overnight star patterns in the heavens with which everyone had become familiar had slipped below their horizon. Their night sky was new and different. It was as though the globe of planet earth had tilted upwards, and the familiar star patterns on their old horizon had slipped below the new horizon. Countries above what is known as, the Tropic of Cancer, reported colder winters, whereas nations in parts of the globe below the Tropic of Cancer, were complaining that their summers were becoming unbearably hot, evaporating water resources above ground and burning up food crops and resources for themselves and their animals, adding further to the misery around the globe.

CHAPTER 16
ICELANDS VOLCANOES WILL ERUPT WITH FAR REACHING CONSEQUENCES

In the year 1918 twenty million people had died from a worldwide influenza epidemic. UK letter post was increased to one and a half penny (in old money). Germany was defeated in the First World War. What was not in the news was a massive volcanic eruption from a volcano in Iceland. It is estimated that the plume rose five miles into the upper atmosphere. The heat caused nearby glaciers to melt. Such eruptions occur in Iceland on a regular eighty year cycle.

The next eruption is now well overdue. What I saw was a more massive eruption, than in the past. I saw a serious problem that will occur continually over the next forty to fifty years. The difference between now and 1918, is that in the twenty first century, aircraft jet engines catch fire or seize up if they suck in hot debris from a volcanic plume. An eruption in Iceland in the present day will close UK airspace, grounding aircraft, and forcing the closure of many airports, because plumes reaching into the upper atmosphere are a danger to air traffic.

I saw the volcanic eruptions in Iceland continuing as a regular event, causing Iceland to build in size to become more like the shape of Japan. The undersea volcano continued to grow from the build up of volcanic ash, until it reached up through sea level to become a feature of Iceland's landscape. The periodic eruptions, and the problems they cause, will have a roll on effect of producing losses of revenue to world airlines, and difficulties for the transportation of any form of fresh or exotic foods.

Devastating Consequences for Africa and Egypt

I saw the dust from Iceland's volcanoes form into a thick black band of dust and sand, covering East and North Africa, fetching a fifty year drought over the whole landmass, and a complete failure of the annual Nile flood. It is difficult to talk about or want to imagine the great catastrophe for human kind that will result.

Devastating Consequences for the North Atlantic Conveyor

Volcanic lather and heat from Iceland's volcanoes exacerbates the melting of glaciers and icebergs, pumping fresh water onto the North Atlantic Conveyor, causing it to sink and slow down, reducing water temperature with consequences for the Northern Hemisphere as far away as Alaska and Scandinavia.

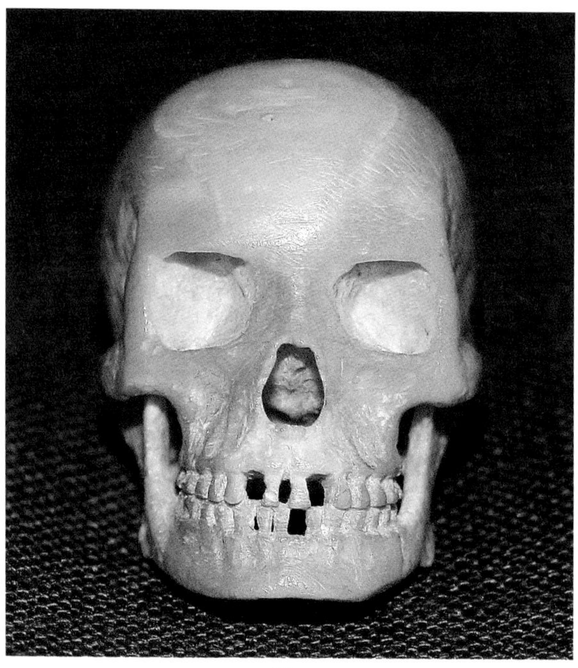

CHAPTER 17

MALDIVES DISAPPEARS UNDER WATER

The strangest sight I saw in the Indian Ocean, were buildings protruding from beneath a calm blue ocean with no solid ground around them. Water reached up to ground floor window level. Everyone appeared to be scurrying from building to building in small boats, distributing water and food being unloaded from a large vessel with Australian Navy markings. I could not discern whether this was the result of a flood, or a permanent inundation of ocean covering the island. I suspect that it is the result of a permanent rise in the level of the ocean.

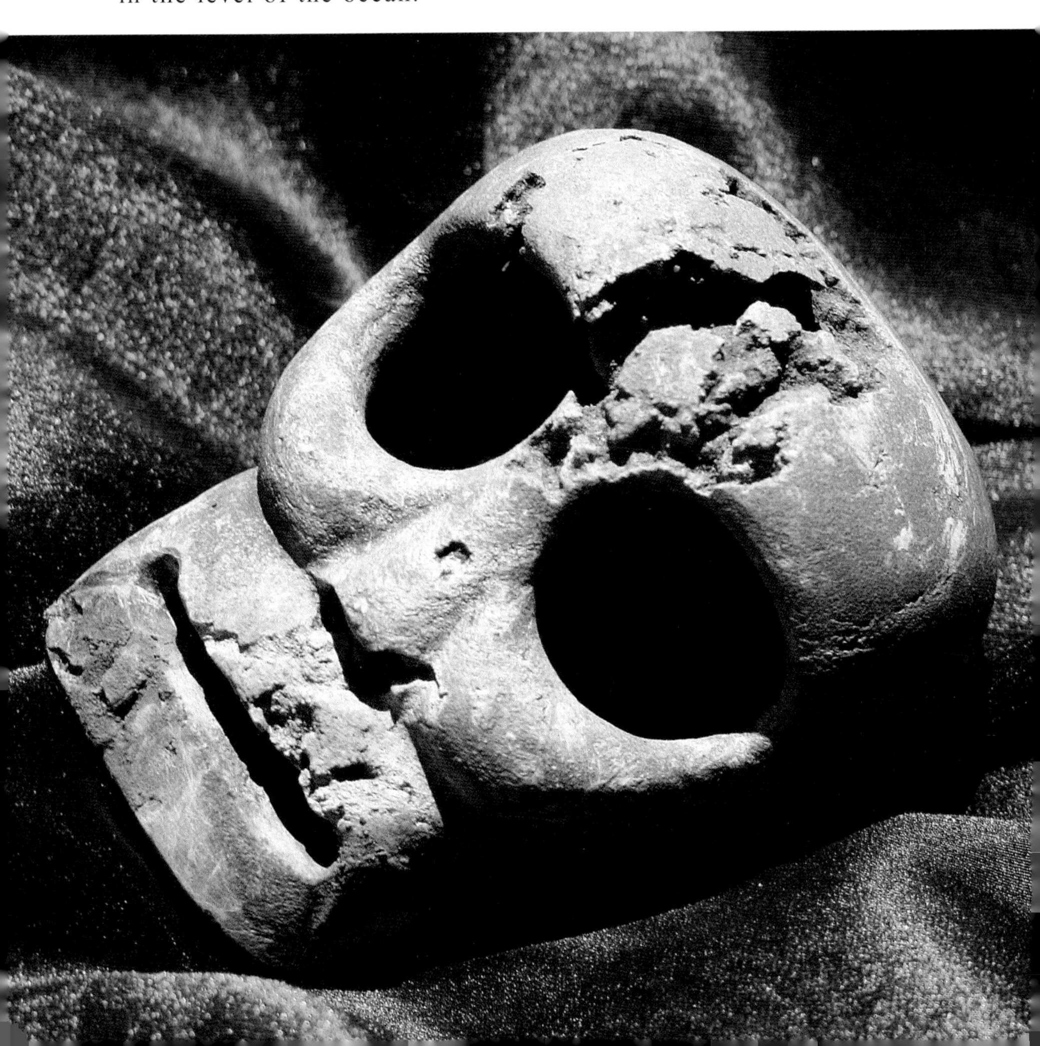

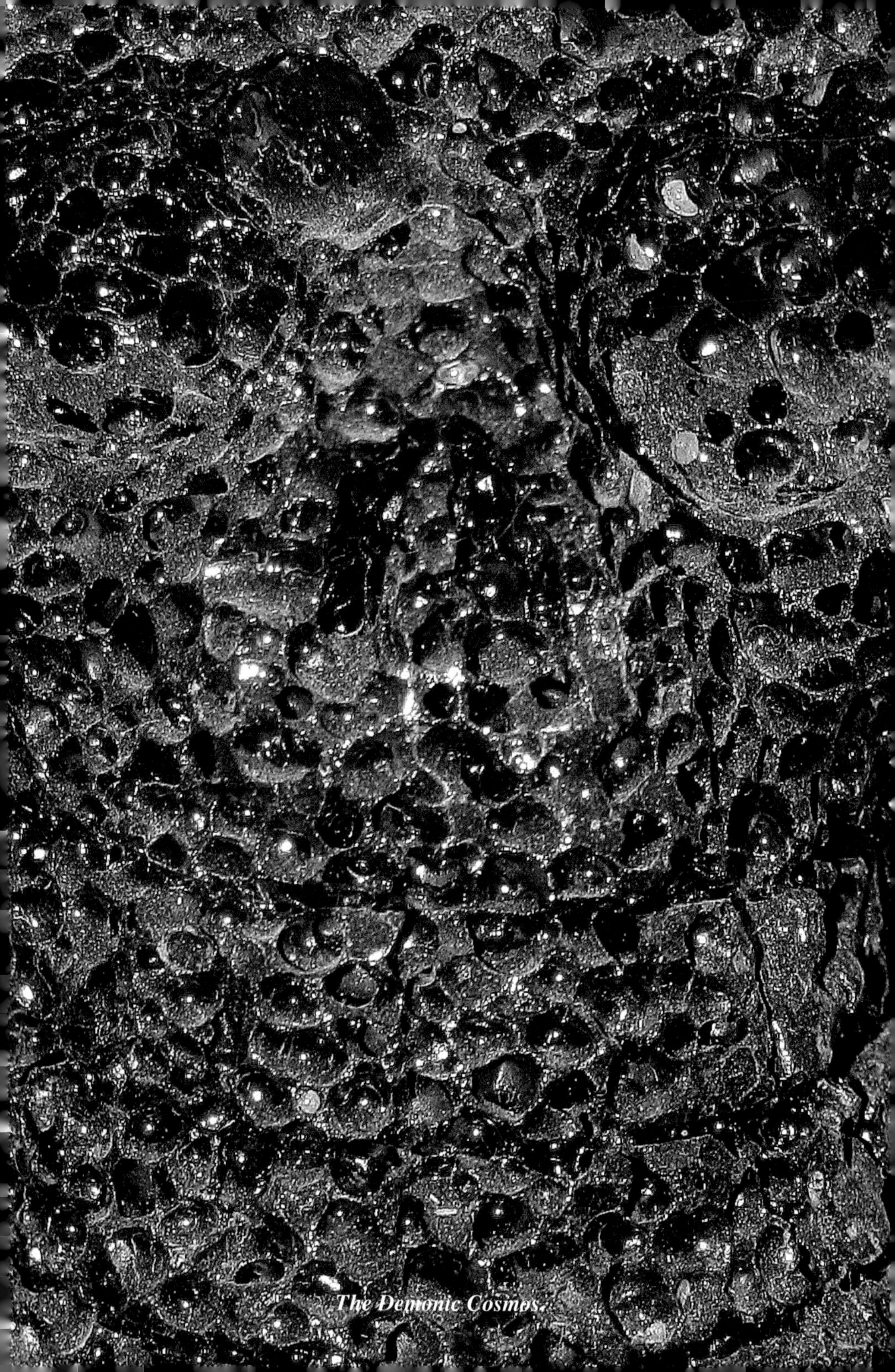

The Demonic Cosmos.

A Tibetan
'Prayer for the World',
placed inside the skull of a Lama
and left in a remote cave in the Himalayas by Craig Allen Rayner

A ROSE BY ANY OTHER NAME

Goddess Mother of the Mountains.
Chomolungmo.
Bathed in Sweet scented Flowers
And green nature Grasses.
Once again blinds us
With the Supernatural

We worship the Sun.
We are the Ancients once again.

My Mandalas glow with new meaning
And Life starts its cycle.
Nature takes its course
And excites us with every
Breath we take.

We are visited by other worlds.
Other creatures.
Travellers it would seem
From time and space.
Eager to breath smell and touch.

They do not know us
But love us and wonder
At our happiness.

We smile.
The Sun shines upon us.
And the children bring us laughter.

Brothers and Sisters.
Our eyes once again
Turn upon this truly spectacular Creation.
We climb her.
We descend her.
We become her.

Your Everest.
Our Chomolungmo.

Sylvia Rayner.

The Last Secrets.

' The Secret of Everest has been solved.

We know now that there is a way to the top.

And we know what that way is.'

John Buchan 1923.

PRAYER FOR THE WORLD

CRAIG ALLEN RAYNER RISKED LIFE AND LIMB CLIMBING INTO A SMALL HIMALAYAN CAVE TO PLACE HIS PRAYER FOR THE WORLD, CARVED ON AN ANCIENT BLOCK, WHICH HE PLACED INSIDE THE SKULL OF A SHAMAN. IT IS CRAIG'S HOPE AND WISH THAT THE NIGHTMARE SCENARIOS PREDICTED IN HIS FATHER RONALD RAYNERS' BOOKS, 'THE VOYAGES OF JOSEPH OF AVALON', 'JOSEPH ESCAPES TO GLASTONBURY', AND 'ALIEN MONK SPIRIT OF NOSTRADAMUS' PREDICTED TO COME TOGETHER IN FUTURE TIME, WILL NOT HAPPEN. HOWEVER, IT IS CRAIG'S FEAR THAT A SHADOW IS BEING CAST BY AN ALLEGORY OF SODOM AND GOMORRAH, AND THAT HIS FATHER HAS BEEN CHOSEN TO BE THE MESSENGER.